The New Testament

and

THE LAW

A NEW TESTAMENT STUDY ON THE VALIDITY OF JEWISH LAW

by Michael W. Marks

Joy Publishing

P.O. Box 9901

Fountain Valley, CA 92708

www.joypublishing.com

New Testament and the Law

A New Testament Study on the Validity of Jewish Law

By Michael W. Marks

© 1999 Michael W. Marks
Shammash Ariel Messianic Congregation
740 W. 15th Street
Pueblo Colorado
(719) 546-8000
Fredteck@aol.com

Published by:

Joy Publishing
P.O. Box 9901
Fountain Valley, CA 92708
www.joypublishing.com

ISBN # **0-939513-36-6** 2nd Edition

Printed in United States of America

TABLE OF CONTENTS

Dedicated to

This book is dedicated to my wife Winnie, the smartest woman in the Universe. Not only can she spell, but she brings out the best in me!

INTRODUCTION

Over the years of my ministry, I have found that there are many techniques used in Biblical investigative problem-solving. For me, it is not enough to simply read a few books and form some kind of an opinion, based solely on someone else's work. That has always seemed to me to be the easy way out because there is no original thought taking place in the mind of the Bible student. It has been my method, over the years, to attack a Biblical subject from an historical, linguistically, and cultural basis, and to record my findings in the form of a "position paper." This project first began as one of those "position papers," so that I might have a record not only of what I believe about the theology of the Messianic Movement, but why and how I came to hold this opinion and to believe the way I do.

In the beginning, it was not my intention for this to become a book. Yet it appears to have grown into one. It is my hope that this study will be useful to those who are dealing with the same questions. Also, in the past few years, as I searched for resources on this topic, I have come to realize that there is not a lot of material available on this subject. What few studies that do exist do not approach the topic from the same "sterile," or narrow position I have used. Because of this "sterile" approach, it seemed good to me to share what I discovered in my studies with others. It appears that wherever I go, there are people who are now asking the same questions that I have had to ask about New Testament Theology and the practices of the Messianic Movement.

2

In developing this study I decided (with a little help from my wife and a few friends) I should write on the theology of Law (Torah) as found in the New Testament. To understand this book, the reader must realize I am writing from a very narrow perspective, that of the New Testament only. This has been done in order to examine the theology and practices of the modern-day Messianic movement and its relationship to Biblical Christendom in light of Christendom's primary source, which is the New Testament. The focus of this book is restricted to what can be discerned and understood about the "LAW" through the writings of the New Testament. This permits the New Testament to speak for itself concerning this subject of "The Law." I have avoided using extra-Biblical material out of fear of tainting the outcome of the study.

So, there are now two purposes that have been assigned to this work. The first is to help those of us who are Messianic come to a greater understanding and appreciation of the fulfillment of the Torah and the Tanach (Old Testament) within the Brit Hadasha (New Testament) and thereby to understand that the New Testament and its 'New Covenant' is not a Gentile book, nor is the New Covenant a Gentile covenant. In fact, there is no book in the Bible that was ever written by a Gentile. (This is not to say that God has not given the Gentiles a place, however. The place of the Gentiles in the Covenant will be explored further on in this study.)

The second purpose is to help the traditional Gentile Church grow in its understanding of the Old Testament and in appreciation of its Jewish roots. In fact, we need to realize that the only legitimate Biblical roots that either the Church, or the Messianic Believer, has are Jewish roots. If we are to be honest, then we will realize that our Christian faith is built on a Jewish book of Jewish Law, with worship centered on a Jewish Messiah who will come back to a Jewish capitol, to sit on a Jewish throne in a Jewish Temple as a Jewish king. I realize that the term 'Jewish' in the last sentence was a bit redundant, but it helped to make my point quite well. If we are to understand the Bible in the context in which it was written, then our understanding must start with an acknowledgment of the Bible's origin.

A.W. Tozer said "Every time a Christian picks up his Bible he is reminded of his debt to the Jews. It is an astonishing thing that multitudes of Bible students and lovers of the truth should calmly overlook their obligation to Israel." Just so there is no confusion, let the reader understand that I believe that the Bible is just one book, not two. It is not, as some have believed, two books, one with a new approach to God and the other with an old outdated truth. As God is One (Echad), so is His book.

The study that is now before you is a New Testament study on the validity of the Law and the Old Testament in the life of the modern Christian. In my twenty-plus years of ministry, I have found that many Christians, and even some ministers, suffer real confusion concerning what part the Old Testament still plays in the life of the Believer. Many mainline denominations even hold to the idea that the only value and purpose the Torah has is historical and poetical, and that it lacks any real legitimacy in governing the life of the modern day Believer.

Yet, in spite of this confusion and supposed out-datedness, many Christians have recently taken up a search for an historical, Biblical lifestyle and have returned to some of the early Jewish traditions and practices as outlined in the Old Testament. And, for some of these Believers, this search has become a driving force, a zealous attempt to rediscover their scriptural roots and heritage. This study will reveal, through the New Testament, answers to questions these searching Believers are asking, questions such as, "Just how Jewish is the Church? Or how Jewish should the Church be?" Another pressing question we will address is, "Just how valid are the practices of the Messianic Movement, especially in respect to returning to the 'old ways' of first century Judaism?"

For many who attend church, the Bible is the undisputed Word of God. At least, that is what most Christians would say when asked. However, over the past several years, with the growth of this new (Messianic) movement, the question of just how much of the Bible is really valid for directing the Christian's life and lifestyle has resurfaced and come into a new light. I am under the impression that most Christians believe that the Old Testament is just that, old and outdated, and no longer useful as a governing force in the life and/or lifestyle of the Believer. Yet, the Messianic Movement has triggered a desire in some Christian Believers to return to the "perceived" roots of the Bible, to what they believe to be a more scriptural lifestyle, and if not that, at least a more Biblically traditional lifestyle.

It is only fair to note that the Messianic movement is not really a new movement in the Church, but one that has cropped up periodically since the writing of the New Testament. There are some people who hold to the view that this current attempt to return to first century Jewish/Christian standards, lifestyle and traditions is a type of legalism. However, it is equally true that those who feel this way may often prove to be legalistic themselves, in their approach to what they call 'acceptable' Christian practices. The subject of whether or not this desire to "return to Messianic roots" constitutes legalism will be discussed within the context of this study, and by the end of the study, the reader should be able to make up his/her own mind on the questions of legalism.

It should also be noted, before we go any further into this book, that this work is not an attempt to exalt modern day Judaism. Though the Jews of today are the descendants of Abraham, the Judaism of today is not the same as Biblical Judaism. Much to the surprise of many non-Messianic Jews, the Messianic Movement and the New Testament both are older than the Orthodox Jewish traditions and the Talmud(s). Like much of the Church, the Jewish community of today has lost its way and has traded its Biblical foundation for the teaching and rules of men.

STUDY GUIDELINES

The primary Bible translation used in this study is the NIV translation. We will be depending heavily upon the original languages in which the Bible is written, so the reader can expect that there will be many word studies. The bulk of these studies will be from the Greek, because this is a study of the New Testament. The texts for the word studies will be supplied by Strong's Exhaustive Concordance, and will be placed into the body of this paper in their entirety. I have also chosen to include the full text of every Scripture that is used, so that each verse may be read in context as part of the study, and to avoid any misunderstanding of the context. Please do not skip over these verses, as they are part of the body of text that we are studying. Some verses may appear in quotation marks and *Italicized* to remind the reader of the origin of a phrase or a word. The emphasized portions of specific Scriptures will be ***underlined and italicized*** . This is to draw attention to the areas of a verse and or text that are to be examined. As you go through this study a regular dictionary may be of some use, even though we will be defining our terms. Definitions of terms have been included in the body of our text and may also be found in the Glossary of Terms.

THEOLOGICAL MISCONCEPTIONS THE ROAD TO ERROR

Biblical interpretation has never been an easy task. There are scholastically-acceptable rules to guide Biblical interpretation which have been developed over hundreds of years. These rules and their process are referred to as Hermeneutics. Unfortunately, these rules of interpretation are not commonly taught in the local church to laymen, and there are differing schools of hermeneutics, each with its own thoughts concerning the rules and their applications. This leaves the average Christian with a problem. Where does he go for instruction in hermeneutics? Either he spends time learning the rules of Biblical interpretation for himself, or he simply trusts his pastors or Bible teachers, who may or may not know how to apply the rules correctly themselves. Since most Christians are not even aware that there ARE rules of interpretation, they are not aware of the difficulties which may arise when the methods of Biblical interpretation are not applied correctly. Incorrect application of the rules of interpretation leads to dangerous misconceptions about the content of the Scriptures.

As we will see, not all Biblical misconceptions, come from confused terminology or because of a difference in schools of Hermeneutics. In fact, the largest problem area we will deal with will be in the area of "Theological Isogesis." Simply put, these problems are due to misconceptions that exist when one has a predetermined, pre-existing theological position on a particular piece of Scripture before Bible "study" ever begins or when one has made "a prioi" assumptions about the interpretation of a scriptural passage.

When pre-existing postulates exist in the mind of the student, the purpose of studying is then reduced (either consciously or unconsciously) to proving or documenting those preconceived positions or teachings. Such so-called study does not leave room for the learning process, as the end results have already been declared. R.C. Sproul states in his book on hermeneutics, <u>Knowing Scripture</u>, that every student of the Bible must maintain the first Law of Biblical interpretation, which is to draw out of the Scriptures, not to read into the Scriptures. In that book, Sproul argues for "an objective understanding of Scripture in which the Biblical interpreter reads without mixing in his own prejudices." Placing one's own prejudice into the interpretation of a Scripture or text is called "Isogesis." In most cases, the practice of Isogesis will equate to poor exegesis. In laymen's terms, that means you will end up with an incorrect or biased interpretation.

There are four basic misconceptions into which much of Christendom's Biblical interpretation falls. These misconceptions may seem subtle at first, however they do pervert the exegesis of Scripture and predetermine the outcome of the study for even the most earnest Bible students. These particular Isogetical misunderstandings are rarely taught as doctrine, but they are frequently expressed in the tools by which interpretations of Scripture are derived. Often they are so subtle and so appealing that the Bible student accepts the faulty tools of interpretation, as well as the faulty interpretation that they derived from the Scripture, without even looking for, or questioning, its scriptural basis. A prime example of poor use of interpretative tools would be the interpretation derived from prophetic passages of Scripture when the student is under the influence that Salt Lake City is the "New Jerusalem."

The First Major Misconception

The issue that feeds into our first major scriptural misconception is two-pronged. The first prong is the un-Biblical teaching that the Biblical-era Jews believed that Israel's redemption could come by good works and the keeping of the Law of Moses. While this is a popular teaching in the Church today, this concept was never taught in Biblical Judaism. The sacrificial system of the Old Testament was established to be a testimony of the sinful nature of man and his inability to redeem himself. Though the Torah had no power to redeem, the Tanach (Old Testament) held out the hope of a Messiah that would come and, at some point in time, redeem the people of God.

So you may ask, just what is it that modern Jews believe concerning faith and works? There are two things for which the modern non-believing (that is, a Jew who does not believe in Jesus) Orthodox or Conservative Jew waits. First, he awaits the rebuilding of the Temple and second, the coming of Messiah. To understand one of the major dilemmas of Judaism today, in relationship to the plan of salvation, we must comprehend the relationship of the Messiah to the Temple. It is true that Orthodox sages have taught that good works, prayer and charity have replaced the necessity for 'sin' sacrifices, and that Messiah will return only when all of the commandments in the Torah are kept. This teaching, though popular, has not been able to alleviate the heartfelt, Biblical need for redemption experienced by the majority of Jews. Therefore, many modern religious Jews still desire to see the Temple rebuilt, believing that without the Temple and the sin offerings, there is no covering for sin, or for the sins of the fathers that have died waiting for the Messiah. And when the offerings can be made, Messiah will have a place to come to, a Temple for His throne.

The truth about Old Testament Biblical Judaism is the truth of Habakkuk 2:4, which teaches that the righteous shall live by *"faith."* This concept of living by faith is so important that it is repeated in the Talmud. (Makkot 23-24) It is in the keeping of the Law, or in the doing of good works, that a man would hope to show or demonstrate that he was a person of faith. In other words, faith leads to keeping the rules, not the other way around. We find this same Jewish teaching today in the New Testament in the book of James, where the Apostle James says, "What good is it, my brothers, if a man claims to have faith but has no deeds? Can such faith save him? Suppose a brother or sister is without clothes and daily food. If one of you says to him, 'Go, I wish you well; keep warm and well fed,' but does nothing about his physical needs, what good is it? In the same way, faith by itself, if it is not accompanied by action, is dead. .... Show me your faith without deeds, and I will show you my faith by what I do."

Now, if the Apostle James is giving us good Biblical theology here, then good works should be a measurable fruit of the Biblical lifestyle. If the idea of a need to perform measurable good works is "too Jewish" by today's Christian standard, then some may consider the Apostle James to be a "legalist!"

The second prong of this misconception is that today, most Christians are taught that "faith" alone is sufficient for conducting a Biblical lifestyle, and that there is no need for outward evidence of faith or acts of obedience that lead to good works. Thus, there is no need for fruit in the form of "good works." By this standard, the believer may (in fact, should) reject any commandment or teaching that calls for the performance of good works, out of fear that it may be legalistic and thus doctrinally incorrect. Following the same logic, then, there is now this nebulous (undefined) freedom in Christ that belongs to the

12

Believer, that is not measurable, and that frees him from the need to bring forth good works. Yet, we are told to judge one another by our fruits. Under such logic, how will that be possible?

So, then our first Theological Isogetical misconception is that many Christians have the (erroneous) idea that the first century Jews believed that they would be saved by works (that is, by following the Law), not by faith, and therefore faith is held to be in opposition to keeping the Law of God. This leads to the perception that Faith and Works are mutually exclusive, and if you have one, you need not (should not, must not) have the other.

The Second Misconception

Our second Theological Isogetical misconception is the idea that all of the Old Testament, (referred to as the "Tanach"), constitutes what many Christians improperly call "The Law." If the commonly-accepted presupposition that Jesus "did away with the Law" is accurate, then, according to this misconception, the entire Old Testament is no longer in effect! This teaching comes from poor instruction as to the structure and the divisions of the Word of God. As far as most people are concerned, the Bible is simply divided into the New Testament and the Old Testament. We, who are called to be teachers of God's Word, must, at some point, teach the Laity about the structure of the Word of God with its various parts. The truth is that the "Law" consists of some specific passages in the Tanach, but the entire Tanach is not "the Law." The Law, or that portion of Scripture commonly known as the Torah, is made up of the first five book of the Bible, those books that are attributed to Moses. From there, the Old Testament Scripture is further divided into "history," "poetry" (sometimes referred to as 'the writings'), and "the prophets." Some schools of thought break it down even much further. (To teach on the structure and the divisions of Bible text would take another complete work in itself, yet which would prove to be invaluable.) In today's modern church, there is much "popular" teaching, but little contextual instruction, and even less teaching in the area of systematic exegesis and Biblical structure. Yet without such instruction we condemn the Bible student to poor interpretational skills.

The Third Misconception

The third Theological Isogetical issue that faces us is the failure of our Bible teachers to consider history, the cultural times and traditions, or the society of the people to which the Scripture was given. When we look into the Bible, we must remember that we are participating in a cross-cultural, cross-historical experience, and that the Bible was not written in context of the Western, Post-Victorian mind set of the 20th century. The failure to correctly translate the Bible through time and culture is as critically dangerous as failing to translate it properly into modern language. It is also essential for the serious Bible scholar to be a student of Biblical history, for without the knowledge of history, the only interpretation that becomes possible is a modern one.

The Fourth Misconception

The fourth, and likely the most dangerous, erroneous Isogetical concept is "Replacement Theology," which is a teaching that we will be discussing in great detail later in this study. It is a very old teaching that runs through much of Christendom and alters one's interpretation of Scripture. Simply put, the teaching says that the Church has become the "New" Israel; the Jews are "out" and the Gentile Christians are "in." This teaching, combined with the idea that the Old Testament is no longer valid, creates an entirely new basis for the Christian Church and its faith. And, if that is not enough, it is also contrary to the very nature of God, Himself, for it creates a God that can and does forget His covenants, abandons His people, and then takes His promises and gifts and gives them to another. It is this author's belief that such a God is not the God of the Bible. Such a God is not the God of Abraham, Isaac and Jacob, for Exodus 2:24 tells us that "God remembered His Covenant with Abraham, with Isaac and with Jacob."

On another note, Replacement Theology creates a real dilemma for students of Biblical prophecy in areas where the Scripture speaks about the rebuilding of the Temple or the people returning to the land of Israel after being in exile. Will it be the Gentile Church which rebuilds the Temple? Will God gather, from the four corners of the earth, the Gentile Church to the land that He promised to their fathers? Much of replacement theology was developed before 1948, and before the restoration of the State of Israel. Of course, at that time, recent prophetical fulfillment's had not yet taken place, and Replacement Theology was thought to be some kind of spiritualized, or metaphorical teaching. (Interestingly enough, most Jews have always known that these prophectical events would actually come to pass. This is seen in the traditional recitation at the close of the Passover seder, "Next year in Jerusalem!" If the replacement theologists are correct, it should be Christendom, not the Jews, who say "Next Year in Jerusalem," and the Church, not the Jews, who will rebuild the Temple. It would be Christians, not the Jews, who have a right to the Land, and Christians, not Jews, who will be the 144,000 witnesses of the book of Revelations.)

TORAH -THE LAW OF GOD

<u>Exodus</u> <u>31:18</u>   When the LORD finished speaking to Moses on Mount Sinai, He gave him the two tablets of the Testimony, the tablets of stone *<u>inscribed</u> <u>by</u> <u>the finger</u> <u>of</u> <u>God.</u>* (NIV)

Students who have studied the major covenants of the Bible will recognize that the Torah is the third covenant that the Lord had made with man. The first covenant was with Noah, with the rainbow as the "sign," and the second with Abraham, concerning his family and the Land that God would give them. What sets this third covenant apart from the others is that this covenant, or contract, was written by the very finger of God. There are those who call themselves Biblical Scholars (both Jewish and Christian) who believe the Torah and the Tanach are nothing but a collection of folk stories. To others, the Bible may be a great book, but it is not divinely inspired nor even historically accurate. For them, the Bible may be just a book of somewhat outdated moral codes. As the author of this study, I believe I should communicate my position on this issue. I believe that "The Law," and every part of the traditionally accepted Bible of Christendom, both New and Old Testament, is God-given, God-spoken, and God-ordained.

<u>Exodus</u> <u>24:3-8</u>   Then Moses went and told the people all *<u>the Lord's</u> <u>words</u> <u>and</u> <u>Laws,</u>* they responded with one voice, "Everything the LORD has said we will do." *<u>Moses</u> <u>then</u> <u>wrote</u> <u>down</u> <u>everything</u> <u>the LORD</u> <u>had</u>*

said. **He got up early the next morning and built an altar at the foot of the mountain and set up twelve stone pillars representing the twelve tribes of Israel. Then he sent young Israelite men, and they offered burnt offerings and sacrificed young bulls as fellowship offerings to the Lord. Moses took half of the blood and put it in bowls, and the other half he sprinkled on the altar.** _Then he took the Book of the Covenant and read it to the people. They responded, "We will do everything the LORD has said; we will obey." Moses then took the blood, sprinkled it on the people and said, "This is the blood of the covenant that the LORD has made with you in accordance with all these words."_

When we speak of "The Law" in Scripture, we are speaking about the first five books of the Bible, that which many scholars call the Torah. The Old Testament, as a whole, is the Tanach (also sometimes referred to as the Pentateuch). More than just tradition, the book of Exodus tells us that Moses wrote these books down as God spoke them to him. Often, uninformed Christians confuse the Torah with what the Jewish community calls the Talmud. The Talmud is considered by many non-Messianic Jews to be the <u>spoken</u> (or Oral) Law of God, whereas the Torah is the <u>written</u> Word of God. Some Jews (not all) hold the two of them in equal estate, believing that together, they constitute God's Word to mankind. However, as we shall soon see, the truth of the matter is that the Talmud is really the Jewish "how-to" commentary on the Torah. We who are Messianic cannot accept the Talmud as a divinely expressed Word of God. There are two basic problems we have with the "Oral Law" that make it unacceptable as a divine work.

#1 Torah Vs Talmud

It is thought by many Orthodox Jewish scholars that the Talmud is based on everything that the Lord had spoken to Moses, but that had not been written down (at the time at Sinai), and from there, this information was passed on by oral tradition. This oral tradition later **was** written down, and become the Talmud. The first argument against the Talmud as a divine Oral Law is, of course, the Torah itself.

Exodus <u>24:3-4</u> When Moses went and told the people all the Lord's words and Laws, they responded with one voice, "Everything the LORD has said we will do." *<u>Moses</u> <u>then</u> <u>wrote</u> <u>down</u> <u>everything</u> <u>the</u> <u>LORD</u> <u>had</u> <u>said.</u>* ... (NIV)

<u>Exodus</u> <u>24:7</u> Then he took *<u>the</u> <u>Book</u> <u>of</u> <u>the</u> <u>Covenant</u>* and read it to the people. They responded, "We will do everything the LORD has said; we will obey." (NIV)

Verses three and four are part of the same text as verse seven, which identifies the Lord's words as the "***<u>Book</u> <u>of the</u> <u>Covenant</u>***" or "The Law." It is in verse four that we understand that the Lord not only gave the covenant, but that Moses was careful to properly record it in its entirety. "***<u>Moses then wrote down everything the LORD had said.</u>***"

In the "Stone Edition" of the Tanach (Old Testament), which is one of the most prestigious works in Orthodox Judaism, Mr. Stone's English translation of this text, from **Exodus 24:4** reads as follows: "Moses wrote down **ALL** the words of Hashem (God)." If Moses really did write them ALL down, then there is no basis for viewing the "Oral Law" or Talmud as a "divine" work, or even for believing that it began with Moses. In the Hebrew text כָּל־דִּבְרֵי means literally ALL WORDS so we must conclude, on the basis of the Torah, that Moses really did give us, in writing, all that the Lord had said.

Exodus 24:4

⁴ וַיִּכְתֹּב מֹשֶׁה אֵת כָּל־דִּבְרֵי יהוה וַיַּשְׁכֵּם בַּבֹּקֶר
וַיִּבֶן מִזְבֵּחַ תַּחַת הָהָר וּשְׁתֵּים עֶשְׂרֵה
מַצֵּבָה לִשְׁנֵים עָשָׂר שִׁבְטֵי יִשְׂרָאֵל: (BHS)

#2 No Historical Text

Allow me a moment to explain about the **Talmuds,** for there are really two major works. One is the Talmud Bavli, most often referred to as the 'Babylonian' Talmud, and the other is the Talmud Yerushalmi, or the *Jerusalem* Talmud. Both are similar in make-up. Though the two Talmuds may find themselves in agreement on the broad strokes of Judaism, the Babylonian Talmud is about three times the size of the Yerushalmi Talmud, and is thought by many to be the authoritative source for the majority of modern Judaism.

Now, as a Messianic, my second problem with the Talmuds derives from the fact there is no historical proof or documentation that shows that any portion of either of the Talmuds existed in any written form before the Babylonian captivity. According to historical sources, it is possible that

20

the formal, written construction of the Talmuds did not even begin until about 150 c.e. (110 years after Messiah), when many of the traditional practices were in danger of extinction because of the Diaspora. In fact, according to the Jewish Encyclopedia, the Jerusalem Talmud was completed around 425 c.e. under Rabbi Johahan Ben Nappaha, and the Babylonian Talmud was not a finished work until 500 c.e. It was completed under Rav Ashi, a noted sage of his time.

This means that the Talmud's' written form may not have come into existence for as much 2500 years AFTER the giving of the Torah. Because of this great gap in time, it is hard to conceive the validity of the Talmud as a divinely-given text. Though I do believe that many of the oral traditions were in place by the first century, the truth is that the Brit Hadasha (New Testament) was gathered and assembled by the year 110 c.e. and thus is an older Jewish text than the Talmud's, and was already 350 years old when the written Talmud's were completed.

I also believe that there is a validity to the Talmud as a historical source, a commentary and as a cultural biography of Judaism, but not as a divine work, equal to the Word of God which is found in the Torah. In conclusion, the problem remains that we cannot get beyond the lack of physical proof that would support the Talmud's existence before the Babylonian captivity or even before the writing of the New Testament. For the non-Messianic religious Jew, the Torah tells what the heart and the commandments of God are, while the Talmud explains some of the ways that the Torah can be lived out.

<u>TORAH</u>

towrah {to-raw'} or torah {to-raw'} from 03384;
1) Law, direction, instruction
1a) instruction, direction (human or divine)
1a1) body of prophetic teaching
1a2) instruction in Messianic age
1a3) body of priestly direction or instruction
1a4) body of legal directives
1b) Law   1b1) Law of the burnt offering
1b2) of special Law, codes of Law

The term "Torah" is found 213 times in the Old Testament and is most commonly translated into English as "commandments" or as "Law." Strong's Concordance defines "Torah" as law, direction and instruction. The term Torah may also be understood to mean teaching, instruction or commandment, as well as Law. We shall soon see that the Laws of the Torah are divided into several different categories and each of these categories were meant to direct a particular aspect of a Jew's life. Much to the interest of the reader, it should be noted that of the four categories that we will cover, only one deals with the Sacrificial system and its Laws.

<u>Torah</u> <u>And</u> <u>The</u> <u>Four</u> <u>Types</u> <u>Of</u> <u>Law</u>

There is a type of theological misconception that most Christians seem to have, one that effects the way that they look at the Torah. It is based on a failure to understand that the Torah is more than just the commandments or the Laws concerning the sacrifices of the Temple. In fact, the

Torah is the least understood portion of the Bible in all of Christendom. The reality of Torah is found in the 613 commandments that are recognized by the Jewish Orthodox Rabbinate. The Torah's 613 Laws can be classified into four major categories for the purpose of study. This is not to say that these are the only acceptable classifications, but for our purpose we will keep it simple. The four classifications are:

1) SACRIFICIAL AND RELIGIOUS LAW
2) CRIMINAL AND CIVIL LAW
3) DIETARY AND HEALTH LAW
4) SOCIAL ORDER

Though some of the commandments may be placed in more than one of these categories, such as the Laws concerning the Sabbath, (which we may identify as both religious and social order commandments), all 613 commandments will be found in at least one of these four major categories.

Sacrificial Laws

The Sacrificial Laws are found throughout the Torah. These are the Laws that tell us what sin is (that is, what constitutes sin), and what the appropriate sacrifice (or payment) for an offense was. However, offerings for sin were not the only sacrificial offerings that were defined. There were other sacrifices to be made as Fellowship Offerings and gifts of praise, as well as gifts of thanksgiving to God. Among these offerings was the עֹלָה

(*olah*), or what most Christian scholars call the "Burnt Offering." This voluntary sacrifice held such importance and was so intensely dedicated that even the ministering priest could not share in it. (Leviticus chapter 1) Another of the sacrifices was a הַמִּנְחָה (*minchah*) or "Meal Offering." The very term itself at one time meant "tribute" and now is used by religious Jews to mean afternoon prayer. Among the voluntary offerings, there was one that would be the forerunner of a celebration that the worshiper would hold, called the זֶבַח שְׁלָמִים (*zevach shelamim*) or the Sacrifice of Well-being, best known as the Peace Offering.

We should note, in order to be historically correct, that sacrifices did not start at Sinai, when the Law was given to Moses. They go as far back as to the time of early Genesis, Chapter four, to the time of Cain and Able. The giving of sacrifices has always been a method of worshipping and honoring God. This has been an expression of worship from the very beginning of time, practiced by a multitude of people groups, not just Jews. From a purely sociological perspective, there has never been a people group on the face of the earth that has not had a sacrificial system of some type. Sacrifices were common to all early cultures, from the Incas and Mayas to early Druids of western Europe. The sacrificial concept did not begin, nor did it end, with the Jews. The point of interest here is that there is a universal knowledge within mankind that has directed expressions of his relationship with his God. Now, if we follow the same vein of thought concerning sacrifices, even the modern Christian Church talks about being sacrificial, yet (except for the Catholic

Eucharist) it has no systematic definition of what that means. In concert with this unfortunate lack of definition, much within the church has been labeled as sacrificial, and yet there is very little actual substance ever being given to God beyond a few mouthed words or a round of applause, and with a little luck, a few dollars. So, while the Jewish sacrificial Laws in the Torah are interesting and informative, they are not unique in the ancient world.

Civil Law

The Civil Laws of the Torah represent the Laws of the Land. They are the Laws that deal with community order, crime, retribution, restitution, and any other event that would require a judge or a civil authority to settle a dispute. Such Laws also dealt with the buying, selling and the treatment of slaves, or land, and the repayment of debt. Among these Biblical Laws dealing with civil and criminal activity, we find the description of the *"cities of refuge."* (Numbers 35:11) The Cities of Refuge were prison cities for those who broke the Civil Law of the Torah. The Civil Laws are the portion of Torah that is meant to create a structure of civil justice that could hold the people together as a society. It may be of some interest to know that, as Americans, our civil and criminal legal systems are built on the Old Testament standard taken directly from these sections of the Torah. It is from this set of Biblical Criminal and Civil Laws that our standards for such things as capital punishment and restitution have been derived. Torah also gives us the distinction between such things as manslaughter and murder. As an American citizen, I do find it a bit ironic that our country, which once claimed a Judeo-Christian heritage, and is now moving away from that Biblical standard, has the Ten Commandments written in stone in the building that houses the highest courtroom in our land, the Supreme Court.

As I noted at the beginning of this section, if we, as Christians, believe that the Civil and Criminal Law of the Torah passed away with the death of Christ, then so has this Biblical standard for how we should live as a society, and so have these Biblically-based Laws which were meant to govern our communities. And, if this is true, then all social order and the Biblical concept of society that God had ordained has passed away also. In that case, a Godly (Biblical) structure for our society is no longer valid. Christians who believe that the Law has "passed away" must ask themselves, "Is our society then to be defined only by the secular world around us?"

Dietary And Health Laws

The Jewish Laws concerning cleanliness, the washing of hands, the identifying of infections, the use of isolation and other related health subjects were well beyond the medical knowledge of the people in the time of Moses. Yet the Lord gave to Israel knowledge that is practiced today by every civilized society on the face of the earth. (As an interesting point of history, if the Gentile Church of the middle-ages had kept the health Laws of the Old Testament during the time of the Black Death [Bubonic Plague], the death toll may have been cut in half.)

The Dietary Laws can often be defined by one word, *kosher*, (in Hebrew called Kashrut). These are the Laws that are concerned with the types of foods that are permissible to eat, the processes of how they are to be stored and how they are to be prepared. A study of the Biblical Dietary and Health Laws is very interesting because of the many modern day health issues. You may note that many health authorities believe that eating kosher is good for you, when kept as a ongoing discipline. However, Kosher means a lot more than just not eating pork or shellfish, it is a true discipline for a healthily lifestyle. Kosher can be defined in two ways. The first is "Rabbinical," and the second is "Biblical." "Rabbinical" refers to keeping Kosher according to strict Orthodox Jewish teaching, found within the Talmud. This type of Kosher holds to the restrictions of the early Rabbis' teachings. Rabbinical Kosher requires that you take as much care in how you prepare foods as what you prepare. In Orthodox homes, meat and dairy items are never served at the same, since such a meal would violate Talmudic teaching. Thus, the proper Rabbinical Kosher home requires two sets of pots and pans, as well as dishes, seeing that the items used to hold meat may never touch the items that are used for dairy. Also, Rabbinical Kosher homes will most likely have two refrigerators, since dairy products and meat may not be stored together.

"Biblical" Kosher is far simpler, as it is simply the keeping of the dietary Laws found within the first five books of the Bible (Torah). These include refraining from eating those foods which are clearly forbidden and are called unclean (i.e. pork, shellfish, scavenger animals, etc.), and those which contain blood.

These dietary Laws are kept by many Conservative Jews and most Messianics, as well as by some other Christian denominations. Biblical Kosher strives to only fulfill the mandates found in the Torah.

The Laws Of Social Order

As stated previously, some commandments can be classified in more than one category. These include many of the Laws addressing religious worship, and religious sacrifice, which may also be found in the Laws that deal with society and Social Order. This is because God, and His Word, is meant to be at the heart of every Jewish home. These Laws govern the family, the roles of men and women, child rearing, parental responsibility, education and so on. Among the Laws of Social Order we find the Laws of the Sabbath, with its regulations in reference to work, and the gathering of the family for the celebrations of God's appointed times, such as the Biblical Feasts.

Other Laws of Social Order deal with the relationship of the community to outsiders (the aliens in the land) and also the welfare system, referred to as the Storehouse. Among the Laws that deal with the Jewish society are some which also pertain to Worship. In the Torah you will find the commandments concerning the annual Feasts and their descriptions as well as instructions on how they were to be kept in the homes and by the community in a corporate manner. Though this may seem strange to us, the Jewish people have always held a sense of collective responsibility as a community for keeping these commandments. Many of these commandments may at first appear to be Religious Laws, yet it is important to understand that the Feasts were held in the home, and not in the Temple. The Laws guided the people through their day-to-day, month-to-month, and year-to-year routine.

As we have seen, the Torah was/is more than just a book of sacrificial rules. It was, and to some still is, the governing force in the lives of people. The Scripture teaches, "...If you obey...", then God will bless the people and the community. (Deuteronomy 8)

JESUS AND THE LAW

In our study of the Law, there will be important verses, and there will be eye-opening verses, and there will be certain critically pivotal verses. It will be these critically pivotal verses that we will have to keep coming back to over and over again, if we are to receive a valid Biblical insight into this subject of the Law and the New Testament. It is very important that the reader understands that these PIVOTAL verses are the foundation of all our interpretation. These pivotal verses will dictate our direction and our understanding for all the others.

In the New Testament, the Apostle Paul speaks more to the issue of the Law and Faith than anyone else, but it is Jesus who gives us the one and only truly Critical and Pivotal Scripture for understanding the Law. Matthew 5:17-18 is that text, through which all other Scriptures and their interpretations must be filtered. Without using **THIS TEXT** as the foundation for interpretation of **all** other Scriptures (on this subject) it would be easy to find oneself pitting the teachings of the Apostle Paul against the teachings of Jesus. I do not believe that the writings of the Apostle Paul will ever contradict the teachings of Jesus. Thus, all of Paul's writings must also be filtered through this text. If we were building a house together, then this text would be our foundation. As good builders, we know that we cannot build outside of the established foundation.

Matthew <u>5:17-18</u> Do not think that I have come to _<u>abolish</u> <u>the</u> <u>Law</u>_ or the Prophets; I have not come to _<u>abolish</u> <u>them</u> <u>but</u> <u>to fulfill</u> <u>them</u>_. I tell you the truth, until heaven and earth disappear, not the smallest letter, not the least stroke of a pen, will by any means disappear from the Law until everything _<u>is</u> <u>accomplished.</u>_ (NIV)

Here, in this very important and foundational Scripture, we will find several defining words, as well as two very unique phrases. To understand the writings of Paul on the Law, you must see them in light of this passage in Matthew, with special emphasis placed on the terminology and language. Paul will explain and teach on the Law, but remember, he never will exceed or go beyond the boundaries that are set here, by this teaching of Jesus on this crucial matter. Once again, let me state that it is critical that the Bible student understands this, for it is often Paul who gets the credit (or should I say the blame) for the destroying, or invalidating the Old Testament Scriptures.

Matthew <u>5:17-18</u> Do not think that I have come to _<u>abolish</u> <u>the</u> <u>Law</u> <u>or</u> <u>the</u> <u>Prophets</u>_; I have not come to _<u>abolish</u> <u>them</u> <u>but</u> <u>to fulfill</u> <u>them</u>_. I tell you the truth, until heaven and earth disappear, not the smallest letter, not the least stroke of a pen, will by any means disappear from the Law until everything is accomplished. (NIV)

Why is this Scripture so important? Because it is here that our Lord Jesus defines His intent concerning the Law of Moses, and also the Prophets. Matthew tells us His intent was not to _"abolish"_ but to _"fulfill"_ the Law and the

Prophets. Please note that verses seventeen and eighteen cover more than just the "Law" that was given to Moses, but also all the Prophets (Haftorah). In fact, it covers the whole of the Tanach (Old Testament). When the Lord grouped the Law and the Prophets together in these verses, He created a bond between them that would not permit any serious Bible student to attempt to separate them (at least in the context of what He came to do with them). In fact, they must be treated in parallel, as if they were a single unit. One might think of them as a type of Biblical "Echad." (oneness) Because of this bond, if one is to be fulfilled, then the other must also be fulfilled simultaneously. If one has passed away, then the other has also passed away.

This brings us to a very serious question. Has all Biblical prophesy been fulfilled? If you, as the reader, believe that there is still some prophecy yet to be fulfilled, then you must also believe that the Law is in existence. For, as you can plainly see, Jesus Himself created a link between the Law, and the Prophets, and He clearly states that they <u>jointly</u> will pass away at some point in time.

It was Jesus who said "Do not think that I have come to _abolish the Law or the Prophets_; I have not come to _abolish them but to fulfill them_." Later when we seek to understand Paul writings on this subject of the Law, we will have to interpret them in light of Jesus' own words here in this verse, as well as his intent. But at this time, however, let us just consider the Lord's usage of two very important words. To increase our understanding of this passage of Scripture we will look at these words and their definitions as described by Strong's Concordance. Our first word study is to be on the term *"abolish."*

<u>ABOLISH</u>

2647 cattalo {kat-al-oo'-o} from 2596 and 3089;

AV - destroy 9, throw down 3, lodge 1, guest 1, come to naught 1, overthrow 1, dissolve 1; 17

1) to dissolve, disunite

1a) (what has been joined together) to destroy, demolish

1b) metaph. to overthrow i.e. render vain, deprive of success, bring to naught

1b1) to subvert, overthrow

1b1a) of institutions, forms of government, Laws, etc, to deprive of force, annul, abrogate,

As we can see, Jesus said that His intent was not to *"destroy, throw down, pervert, dissolve, disunite or demolish"* the Law or the Prophets. Rather, He came to *"fulfill"* them. So, what do we do with the popular Christian teaching/idea/phrase that says "the Law has passed away"? If indeed, it has been done away with, then there is nothing to *"fulfill."* But, if the Law still remains, then let us continue to remember that Paul's writings on the Law must be interpreted and confined within Matthew 5:17-18. Jesus said that he has not come to abolish the Law or the Prophets. Now let us define our second vital term *"fulfill"* using Strong's Concordance.

FULFILL

4137 pleroo {play-ro'-o} from 4134;

1) to make full, to fill up, i.e. to fill to the full

1a) to cause to abound, to furnish or supply liberally

1a1) I abound, I am liberally supplied

2) to render full, i.e. to complete

2a) to fill to the top: so that nothing shall be wanting to full measure, fill to the brim

2b) to make complete in every particular, to render perfect

2b2) to carry through to the end, to accomplish, carry out, (some undertaking)

2c) to carry into effect, bring to realization, realize

2c1) of matters of duty: to perform, execute

2c2) of sayings, promises, prophecies, to bring to pass, ratify, accomplish

The use of this Greek word helps us to realize that Jesus came to make the Law *"abound, to make full, to render perfect, to carry through to the end, and to bring to realization."* In simple terms, He was the one who would *"make full"* or to *"bring to realization"* the fullness of the Law. However, let us not make the mistake of thinking that, once brought to *"fullness,"* it becomes obsolete. There is going to be a time when Law will pass away, but until that time comes, Jesus remains the fulfillment of the Law because the Law remains.

So, here is a question we must consider, "When will the whole Law pass away?" If we will continue to read in the same passage in Matthew, the time of the Law's passing away is explained and made clear to us. It is Jesus who declares the conditions and events surrounding the time when the Law will come to an end.

Matthew 5:18 **I tell you the truth, _until heaven and earth disappear,_ not the smallest letter, not the least stroke of a pen, will by any means disappear from the Law until _everything is accomplished_.**

Let us consider those two very important statements concerning the time when the Law would pass away. The first phrase for our examination is _"Heaven and Earth will pass away_ (disappear) _before one_ Yud (the smallest letter), _or the least stroke of a pen, disappears from the Law."_ Please allow me to ask you, when does the heaven and earth disappear? To discern when the Torah will disappear, we must answer this question. When does the heaven and earth disappear? The Apostle Peter gives us the answer to this question and the timing of the Law's disappearance:

2 Peter 3:12-13 .... as you look forward to the _day of God_ and speed its coming. That day will bring about the destruction of the heavens by fire, and the elements will melt in the heat. But in keeping with his promise we are looking forward to a new heaven and a new earth, the home of righteousness. (NIV)

Now we see that, until the _"day of God,"_ or what is sometimes called _"the Day of the Lord,"_ the Law will not pass away. We know then, that all of Paul's writings were developed in the context that the Law had not yet passed away, nor was it about to pass away. That this would only happen after the "Day of the Lord." However, this passing away still is different than what is *"fulfilled."*

The second proof of the Law's disappearance will be when, as Matthew stated, *"everything is accomplished."* This raises an interesting question. Can something be fulfilled and yet not complete? Let us hold this question in mind as we do our word study and define this all-important word *"accomplished."*

<u>ACCOMPLISH</u>

1096 ginomai {ghin'-om-ahee}
1) to become, i.e. to come into existence, begin to be, receive being
2) to become, i.e. to come to pass, happen
2a) of events
3) to arise, appear in history, come upon the stage
3a) of men appearing in public
4) to be made, finished
4a) of miracles, to be performed, wrought
5) to become, be made

In Matthew 5:18, we are told *"not the least stroke of a pen, will by any means disappear from the Law until everything is accomplished."* This word *"accomplished"* is far different in its meaning than our word *"fulfilled."* The difference is that the word *"accomplished"* implies a conclusion, that the Law will come to a point in time when it will be finished, or done, and therefore obsolete. The word *"fulfilled"* means to bring to it highest point of being, to its apex.

If we put all these factors together, then we must come to the understanding that through the work of Jesus Christ, the Law was raised to its highest standard in *"fulfillment"* and yet did not pass away. But we also know that there is a time when it will pass away, because all things will be *"accomplished."* This, then, raises a question, in the form of a riddle. What is being fulfilled and yet not completed? In order to discover the truth and answer to this riddle we need to once again look closely at Jesus' statement, *"Do not think that I have come to <u>abolish</u> <u>the Law</u> <u>or the Prophets</u>;"* If you guessed that the answer to the riddle is "prophecy" then you are correct. The Law, and Biblical prophecy, will come to accomplishmcnt, conclusion and closure, at the same time. It was Jesus' statement that tied them together for all time and only He can bring them to their apex.

<u>Matthew</u> <u>5:19</u> Anyone who breaks one of the least of these <u>*commandments*</u> and teaches others to do the same will be called least in the kingdom of heaven, but whoever practices and teaches <u>*these*</u> <u>*commands*</u> will be called great in the kingdom of heaven. (NIV)

There is a major difference in something that is *"fulfilled"* or completed, and something that has been abandoned or obsolete. If verse nineteen is read in context with seventeen and eighteen, and in light of our understanding of Jesus' previous words, then we must ask, "Is verse nineteen a warning for those would abandon the Law completely?" Strong's Concordance tells us that the Greek word for commandment in this Scripture is *entole (en-tol-ay')*, which means an *order, command, precept, injunction.* Strong's also says it means *ethically used of the commandments in the Mosaic Law or Jewish tradition.* Though it is not a salvation issue, the keeping of the commandments does appear to be high on the Lord's preferred agenda. The truth concerning the importance of the Law may yet be discovered by knowing the reason for the Law's existence.

THE LAW AND ITS PURPOSE

Galatians 3:19 *What, then, was the purpose of the Law?* **It was added because of transgressions until the Seed to whom the promise referred had come.**

The Apostle Paul wrote more about the Law than any other New Testament writer. This is not strange, seeing that Paul was well educated, as a Pharisee, under the teaching of the great Gamaliel, and was knowledgeable in both the Torah and in the oral traditions of his time (pre-Talmud). When Paul is speaking about the Law, he is always careful to speak of it in the most respectful tones, realizing that what he is commenting on is the Word of God. Such respect reminds us that we, too, must handle the Word of God with great care. Paul's comprehension of the Law was that of an expert, as a Pharisee. It is this expertise that will help us to understand the purpose of the Law. To grasp the reason for the Law, we must realize that it was created to be a response to transgression, as an instrument to hold mankind in check until the coming of the "Seed" (the Messiah, Galatians 3:16) that was promised through Abraham.

Although I do not wish to throw the reader for a theological loop, I must point out that this thought raises a new question. If the Law was put into place "Until the coming of the Seed" (Messiah) and it was meant to hold mankind in check, to which coming of the Messiah does this verse refer?

Was it the first coming, in which He is portrayed as the Lamb of God who is to take away the sins of the world as an offering for sin? Or, will it be the second coming, where he is the Lion of Judah and He sets up His kingdom, and will rule with a rod of iron over all the earth? Some believers would answer the first, because we live in the time of grace. If that is true, then the Law has passed away, and with it any concept of what sin is has also passed away, and there can be no more sin. If we say the second coming, then there is a legal basis (as well as a real necessity) for His right to rule and for the idea that He will rule with a rod of iron. Whichever it may be, the fact is that the Law was a response to transgression, one that was put into place until the time of the Lord's coming.

<u>Romans</u> <u>3:19-20</u>   Now we know that whatever the Law says, it says to those who are under the Law, so that every mouth may be silenced and the whole world held accountable to God. Therefore no <u>one</u> <u>will</u> <u>be</u> <u>declared</u> <u>righteous</u> in his sight by observing the Law; <u>rather, through the Law we become conscious of sin.</u> <u>(NIV)</u>

Again we ask, "What is the purpose of the Law? Why was it created?" There are two revelations that this text could unfold for us. The first is that *"no one will be declared righteous"* by observing the Law. The second is that, because of the Law, we become *"conscious"* of what sin is, and that the whole world is held accountable to God concerning sin. Though this Scripture speaks very plainly about the fact that no one would be declared righteous by simply *"observing"* the Law, the purpose for the Law is that we could become *"conscious"* of our sin because of the Law. Paul, the Pharisee, not only tells us here what the Law can do, but also what it cannot do.

In reference to the matter of the consciousness of sin, the whole world, and not just the Jew, is held accountable to God for acts of sin that are described in the Law. (Speaking from a purely non-Biblical, but sociological frame of reference, it is fascinating to note that there has never been a people group that has not had some form of worship to a god, or gods. And, in the context of that worship, every group has had a system of Laws which defined right and wrong. Each society's concept of good and evil is based on that society's understanding of who God is and what God required of the people. From the same sociological perspective, we should note that every society has fallen into extinction based on internal decay. This decay has taken place when man breaks whatever "god" Laws the society has established. This has proven to be true from the ancient Greeks to modern day man.) The Apostle Paul's statement in Romans 1:20 seems to support the idea that the whole world is without an excuse and is accountable to God for sin. *" For since the creation of the world God's invisible qualities - his eternal power and divine nature - have been clearly seen, being understood from what has been made, so that men are without excuse."* By this Scripture we know that God has revealed His divine nature in creation and that through that creation, mankind has understood that God is. Because of this understanding, every society has established a code of laws that defines lawlessness. Thus, the Scripture says no one has an excuse.

However, it is in Paul's statement "*... rather, through the Law we become conscious of sin.*" that he has exposes the purpose for which the Law was created. With a word study from Strong's, we will realize just how deep this "conscious" understanding of sin runs.

<u>CONSCIOUS</u>

1921 epiginosko {ep-ig-in-oce'-ko} AV. - know 30, acknowledge 5, perceive 3, take knowledge of 2, have knowledge of 1, know well 1

1) to become thoroughly acquainted with, to know Thoroughly

1a) to know accurately, know well

2) to know

2a) to recognize

2a1) by sight, hearing, of certain signs, to perceive who a person is

2b) to know i.e. to perceive

2c) to know i.e. to find out, ascertain

2d) to know i.e. to understand

Now, let us rewrite the verses here in Romans, using the definition for the word "*conscious*" as it appears in the Strong's Concordance. In doing this we may get a better picture of the purpose of the Law. With the suggested changes in these verses it could then read:

<u>Romans 3:19-20</u> (RE-WRITTEN) "Now we know that whatever the Law says, it says to those who

are under the Law so that every mouth may be silenced and the whole world held accountable to God. Therefore no one will be declared righteous in his sight by observing the Law; rather, through the Law we become able to _recognize_ _and_ _perceive_ _and_ _even_ _become_ _thoroughly_ _acquainted_ _with_ _sin._" (NIV)

We now come to understand that the purpose of the Law is not to "_declare_" righteousness, but, in truth, the very purpose of the Law is to prove just the opposite. It proves or exposes our unrightousness; it reveals the unholy state of our lives. Paul tells us that "_no one will be declared righteous in his sight by observing the Law._" Paul can say that with all confidence, not because he is this great Pharisee and understands the ins and outs of the Law. It is because he knows that was not the purpose of the Law. The Greek word in this text says to be "_conscious of sin_" is to be "_thoroughly acquainted with_" sin . This is what the Law was created to do, it was to unmask our sin nature. It is because of the Law that we know and understand and are certain of what sin is. Apart from the Law, how would we know? The truth is, we would not know what sin is, and would be eternally condemned to Lawlessness through ignorance. The Jewish New Testament puts it best when it says, "_For in his sight no one alive will be considered righteous on the ground of legalistic observance of Torah commands, because what Torah really does is show people how sinful they are._" (Romans 3:20)

Romans 4:14-15 For if those who live by Law are heirs, faith has no value and the promise is

worthless, *because Law brings wrath. And where there is no Law there is no transgression.* *(NIV)*

Now, let us test this idea that the Law still exists for the New Testament believer. Here is a test question for you. Have you ever known someone to use the term "under conviction," as in reference to the work of the Holy Spirit? I hope most of us have heard that phrase at some point in time. If one is "under conviction," by what authority does the Holy Spirit bring about that conviction, except by that of the Law? What was called sin in the Old Testament is still called sin in the New. The element, or property, that defines what sin is has not changed (the Law), and neither has the authority changed by which we are convicted. What has changed is how we may respond to conviction. Now, without the Law, there is no authority to bring about a conviction that will institute change, because "*where there is no Law there is no transgression.*" Paul, in Romans, is telling us that the "Law" is the only tool that defines transgression. In fact, where there is no Law, there can be no sin. In essence, the Holy Spirit is the agent of the "Law." The question now arises, "Does the Law bring wrath?" YES, on all who are Law-breakers. Paul makes several very serious statements about *wrath, fear, rebellion and lawbreakers* in Romans Chapter thirteen. This proves not only to be true in God's Kingdom, but is just as true in your home town. If you break the Law by speeding, and get caught, then you face the wrath of the court and its judge, all according to the just Laws of the land. Do you think the Kingdom of God is any different?

44

1 John 3:4 *Everyone who sins breaks the Law; in fact, sin is Lawlessness.*

One might even say that without the Law, there is no need, or reason, for grace. In fact, without the Law, grace would have no purpose. Once again, without a definition of Lawlessness (sin), on what shall we be convicted? The Scripture tells us that the work of the Holy Spirit is to convict the world of sin (John 16:8). If there is no Law, then on what will the Holy Spirit base conviction? When there is no conviction, then what is the need or purpose of grace? The Scripture tells us we are saved by grace, through faith, after we have been convicted, and after we have confessed that we are Lawless transgressors.

Romans 7:7-14 *What shall we say, then? Is the Law sin? Certainly not! Indeed I would not have known what sin was except through the Law.* **For I would not have known what coveting really was if the Law had not said, "Do not covet." But sin, seizing the opportunity afforded by the commandment, produced in me every kind of covetous desire.** *For apart from Law, sin is dead.* **Once I was alive apart from Law; but when the commandment came, sin sprang to life and I died. I found that the very commandment that was intended to bring life actually brought death. For sin, seizing the opportunity afforded by the commandment, deceived me, and through the commandment put me to death.** *So then, the Law is holy, and the commandment is holy, righteous and good. Did that which is good, then, become death to me? By no means! But in order that sin might be* _recognized as sin, it produced death in me through what was good, so that through the commandment sin might become utterly sinful. We know that the Law is spiritual; but I am unspiritual,_ sold as a slave to sin. (NIV)

Romans 7:16 And if I do what I do not want to do, _I agree that the Law is good. (NIV)_

Romans, Chapter seven, reveals with clarity the very nature and the purpose of the Law. The nature of the Law is Holiness, while its purpose is to reveal un-holiness. If the nature of the Law is light, then what it exposes is darkness, because that is what is contrary to the nature of light.

In this passage, Paul has expressed how he came to knowledge of the deadliness of his sin, through an understanding of the righteousness of the Law. It is through this knowledge that Paul understood that he was dead in, and because of, his sins. If we come to the same understanding, that the purpose of the Law is to make us _"conscious"_ of sin, then it is at this point that the Law has _"fulfilled"_ its purpose in us. Personally, I believe most people oppose the Law not because it appears to be outdated or is some how unscriptural for modern man, but because it is a source of discomfort, due to the desire not to have to face their own sins or to face the God who gave the Law. To quote the Apostle Paul on this matter, _"We know that the Law is spiritual; but I am unspiritual, sold as a slave to sin."_

<u>Galatians</u> <u>3:23-24</u> **Before this faith came, we were held prisoners by the Law, locked up until faith should be revealed.** ***<u>So</u> <u>the Law</u> <u>was</u> <u>put</u> <u>in</u> <u>charge</u> <u>to</u> <u>lead</u> <u>us</u> <u>to</u> <u>Christ</u> <u>that</u> <u>we</u> <u>might</u> <u>be justified</u> <u>by faith</u>***.

I do not like to use the King James version of the Bible very often because of the language difficulties, but in these verses, I found it to be quite enlightening. As expressed in the KJV, the following verse may help to develop our understanding of God's intentional relationship between the Law and the believer.

<u>Galatians</u> <u>3:23-24</u>   **But before faith came, we were kept under the Law, shut up unto the faith which should afterwards be revealed. Wherefore the Law was *<u>our</u> <u>schoolmaster</u> <u>to</u> <u>bring</u> <u>us</u>* unto Christ, that we might be justified by faith. (KJV)**

The purpose of the Law is to be our spiritual *schoolmaster*. For those who have not been educated in a private or parochial school system, the term schoolmaster may not hold much meaning beyond that of a simple teacher. The schoolmaster, by the old English standard, is more than just a teacher; the schoolmaster is responsible for the well-being and development of the student in all aspects of life, as well as the student's education. The Jewish New Testament puts it this way: *"Accordingly, the Torah functioned as a <u>custodian</u> until the Messiah came, so that we might be declared righteous on the ground of trusting and being faithful."* The term here for custodian is not that of a janitor, but that of a legal guardian, (schoolmaster) who once again is responsible for the development of another individual until he or she reaches the age of maturity. There are some who will say that we (that is, the collective church) have reached this time of maturity. However, the problem may be that we as <u>individuals</u> have not found this maturity. Each new generation, and each new believer, must face the schoolmaster since we do not learn, nor are we redeemed, by osmosis. When the lessons of the Law are fully completed within us, then we recognize our sin and our need for grace. It is then, out of our need for grace, faith is born with in us. This is why Jesus could say, in Matthew 5:17-18, *"Do not think that I have come to abolish the Law or the Prophets; I have not come to abolish them but to fulfill them."* When understanding of the Law and the concept of what sin is come to maturity in us, then so does our knowledge of our need for a Savior- Redeemer.

THE LAW OF SIN AND DEATH

Ezekiel 18:4 For every living soul belongs to me, the father as well as the son -- both alike belong to me. ***The soul who sins is the one who will die.*** (NIV)

In our study of the Torah, we have found that there are four broad classifications of the Laws of God. Within several of these classifications (Civil and Criminal Law, and the Sacrificial Religious Laws) there exists the possibility of committing a <u>capital</u> offense. Violating one of these Laws could result in the forfeiture of one's life, (physical, spiritual, or both) if one was convicted of the violation. Ezekiel 18:4 is a declaration of God's absolute sovereignty in dealing with His creation, as well as how He views sin. As God, He alone holds the power of life and death. In Hebrews 10:1, Paul tells us that the Law is a "typology" or a *"shadow"* of things that are to come. If we know that the Law is a typology, and if we realize that the earthly Torah has Laws within it that carry a penalty which has the power to take a man's life, then we must also realize that there is an absolute, and yet spiritual Law that ends in a form of eternal death. This punishment will be for those whose sin is the rejection of Jesus as the Messiah, or for those who chose to live their lives as perpetual lawbreakers. We must realize that the Laws of Sin and Death are as real and as binding and as active for "New Testament" believers as they were for Old Testament believers. As an example, a case in point in the book of Acts tells us of a married couple who attempted to lie to God, and who, because of that lie, forfeited their lives.

Acts 5:9 Peter said to her, "How could you agree to test the Spirit of the Lord? Look! The feet of the men who buried your husband are at the door, and they will carry you out also." (NIV)

Just what was the real crime here that cost them their lives, you may ask? The offense that took place against God is found in the Law, in the book of Deuteronomy:

Deuteronomy 19:18-20 The judges must make a thorough investigation, and if the witness proves to be a liar, giving false testimony against his brother, then do to him as he intended to do to his brother. You must purge the evil from among you. The rest of the people will hear of this and be afraid, and never again will such an evil thing be done among you. (NIV)

Did they die because they made God angry or was it because they broke the Law of the Torah and bore false witness before the Lord? There are many Christians that simply believe that this coupled died because they dared to anger God. The truth is, they died because they broke the Law.

Acts 5:3 Then Peter said, "Ananias, how is it that Satan has so filled your heart that _you_ _have_ _lied_ _to_ _the_ _Holy_ _Spirit_ and have kept for yourself some of the money you received for the land?" (NIV)

Ananias and his wife did not die because they decided to keep some of the money from the sale of their property. They died because they violated the Law of God which forbade baring false witness, and because, for whatever reason, they chose not to avail themselves of the Grace available to them through repentance.

We must grasp that the concepts of the Laws of Sin and Death are spiritual, and therefore also eternal. They are as applicable in this world as they will be in the next. It is the Apostle Paul who said, *"For the word of God is living and active, sharper than any double-edged sword, it penetrates even to dividing soul and spirit, joints and marrow; it judges the thoughts and attitudes of the heart."* (Hebrews 4:12). Why use such a powerful analogy as a sword unless it is, in fact, far more applicable than most of us dare to admit.

Romans 7:23-25 **but I see another Law at work in the members of my body, waging war against the Law of my mind and making me a prisoner of the *Law of sin* at work within my members. What a wretched man I am! Who will rescue me from this body of death? Thanks be to God - through Jesus Christ our Lord! *So then, I myself in my mind am a slave to God's Law, but in the sinful nature a slave to the Law of sin.***

In Paul's letter to the Romans he confesses his *"wretched"* state and the hopelessness of his life being trapped in the sin that was exposed to him by the Law. In the realization of his miserable and hopeless state, he praises God for the salvation that has come through Jesus Christ, our Lord. Note, however, the last line here. Paul says that he is a slave to God's Law on one hand, and a slave to sin on the other. Paul struggled, like so many of us today, with his two natures, one bound to the Law of Sin and Death, and the other to the Law of the Spirit of Life. Yet either way he is bound to one of these Laws.

Romans 8:2 because through Christ Jesus _the Law of the Spirit of life_ set me free from the _Law of sin and death_. (NIV)

We read, in Ezekiel 24, that the "_soul that sins dies_." Though this may seem harsh, it is the righteous Law of God that requires that a life be given for the payment of sins. So many of today's preachers tell us that salvation is free, but the truth is, it is not "free." If I say that it is free, how do I account for the fact that the Law required (and still requires) a life as payment for transgressions? If it is free, then for what did Jesus sacrifice himself? If I accept this salvation, how can I discount the fact that I must give my life for God's service? Even the Torah teaches me a "_life for a life!_" (Exodus 21:23-25). In the New Testament, Jesus teaches us in the gospel of Luke, _"If anyone would come after me, he must deny himself and take up his cross daily and follow me. For whoever wants to save his life will lose it, but whoever loses his life for me will save it._" Now, let us be honest, does that sound like it is free to you? How about that part of the Scripture that says: "_... he must deny himself and take up his cross daily and follow me,_"?

What we do become free from is the Law of Sin and Death, but we are not free to go along on our merry way. Though the redemption offered through Christ may not be free (as some teachers make it out to be) it is freely given to those who would receive it. And even though it is not free, it is still the best bargain in the universe, as well as man's only redemption.

Today, many Christian believers have a mentality that says that God requires nothing of them, and in return God wants to bless them for simply acknowledging His existence. The cry of the modern American Church is "Serve me, serve me, oh my God." In the last few years, this very popular teaching has gained a lot of support from pulpits around the world. Of course, the only real problem with it is that it is not found in the Scriptures of the Bible.

<u>Exodus</u> <u>21:23-25</u> But if there is serious injury, <u>*you*</u> <u>*are*</u> <u>*to*</u> <u>*take*</u> <u>*life*</u> <u>*for*</u> <u>*life,*</u> eye for eye, tooth for tooth, hand for hand, foot for foot, burn for burn, wound for wound, bruise for bruise.

I believe if we just took ten seconds of honesty, and if the truth were known, it is this verse that strikes fear in the hearts of most believers today. The real issue with the Law may not be one of legalism, but the very idea of God's <u>right</u> to retribution and restitution. This may be what really sends us into a panic, not the concept of legalism. The fear comes when, in our heart of hearts, each one of us may have to acknowledge the truth that he is a sinner. When we speak of having been forgiven, it does not mean that the

Creator of the universe just blew it off, and forgot about our sin. The Lord God does not wink at sin, as if to let it casually slide by. The Law declares the price for sin, as well as the price for redemption. The Torah says *"But if there is serious injury, you are to take life for life, eye for eye, tooth for tooth, hand for hand, foot for foot, burn for burn, wound for wound, bruise for bruise."* And it is this price that the Lord Jesus paid on our behalf, so that we might come to learn about His mercy and grace. Here we see the love of God in Christ Jesus, and His sacrifice has proven the greatness of His Love. With that great sacrifice, was our salvation free? Or was it bought and paid for?

<u>Romans</u> <u>12:1</u> Therefore, I urge you, brothers, in view of God's mercy, <u>*to offer your bodies as living sacrifices,*</u> holy and pleasing to God - this is your spiritual act of worship. (NIV)

Paul teaches us that we are to die to ourselves and to live as to Christ. When Paul speaks of himself in Galatians 2:20, he says *"I have been crucified with Christ and I no longer live, but Christ lives in me. The life I live in the body, I live by faith in the Son of God, who loved me and gave himself for me."* Paul is teaching us by his example how we are to keep the verses in Exodus 21:23-25. It is with a *"life for a life."* Jesus' life was given, now my life is to be given. In the matter of *"pick up of your cross deny yourself and follow me daily,"* it is still a *"life for a life."* King David said, in Psalm 49:7-8, *"No man can redeem the life of another or give to God a ransom for him. The ransom for a life is costly, no payment is ever enough."* Therefore, as we study the *"Law of sin and death"* we need to remember that salvation only appears to be free.

Now, let us review this subject with the words of Jesus and then with those of the Apostle Paul:

<u>Luke 9:23-25</u> Then he said to them all: "If anyone would come after me, *<u>he must deny himself and take up his cross daily and follow me. For whoever wants to save his life will lose it, but whoever loses his life for me will save it.</u>* What good is it for a man to gain the whole world, and yet lose or forfeit his very self?" (NIV)

<u>Romans 6:18</u> *<u>You have been set free from sin and have become slaves to righteousness.</u>*

As we previously noted, there are those who think that because Jesus died for our sins and liberated us from death, we are free to go. But here is the truth of the matter: though you are free from one master you now have another. Let me quote the modern poet and song writer, Bob Dylan, who said, "You got to serve somebody. It may be the Lord above or the Devil below, but you got to serve somebody."

When the majority of Christendom thinks about the Law, it is always in negative connotations. This is most likely due to the fact that we continue to think with a western-world Post-Victorian mindset rather than that of the Jewish mindset. That is why verses like First Timothy 1:8 are often overlooked and why we refuse to understand the process of the Law itself.

1 Timothy 1:8   We know that *the Law is good if one uses it properly.*

Romans 8:2-4 .... because through Christ Jesus *the Law of the Spirit of life* set me free from the Law of sin and death. For what the Law was powerless to do in that it was weakened by the sinful nature, God did by sending his own Son in the likeness of sinful man *to be a sin offering*. And so he condemned sin in sinful man, *in order that the righteous requirements of the Law might be fully met* in us, who do not live according to the sinful nature but according to *the Spirit.* (NIV)

For the *"Law of Sin and Death"* to be *"fulfilled"* (that is what Jesus said he came to do (Matthew. 5:17-18), then a life would be required as the payment under the Law (which payment He Himself paid). For Jesus to establish the New Law, i.e. the *"Law of the Spirit of Life,"* he would have to first *"Fulfill"* the *"Law of Sin and Death."* New laws are built upon the foundation of the established older ones, so one might say that Law is built upon Law. The Law of the Spirit of Life exists only because the Law of Sin and Death exists.

Matthew 20:28 .... just as the Son of Man did not come to be served, but to serve, and to give his life as a *ransom* for many. (NIV)

<u>RANSOM</u>

3083 lutron {loo'-tron} from 3089; AV - ransom
1) the price for redeeming, ransom
1a) paid for slaves, captives
1b) for the ransom of life
2) to liberate from misery and the penalty of their
   Sins

It is in the completion of old Laws that the new ones can be created. So, the *"Law of the Spirit of life"* is dependent on the *"Law of Sin and Death."* Without defining sin, there can be no definition for Grace. *"The Law of the Spirit of Life"* has its foundation in the Torah in the Laws referred to as the Laws of Redemption, located in Exodus and Leviticus. However, the *"Law of the Spirit of Life"* exceeds them, because it is an eternal Law, not just a temporal one (Romans 8:1-2). The temporal Laws of the Torah will, in time, pass away with the heavens and the earth.

<u>Leviticus</u> <u>25:48-49</u> he retains the right of redemption after he has sold himself. *<u>One</u> <u>of his</u> <u>relatives</u> <u>may</u> <u>redeem</u> <u>him</u>*: An uncle or a cousin or any blood relative in his clan may redeem him.

Jesus had to become as a man in order to redeem mankind, for our salvation is based on the Biblical Laws of Redemption. He is referred to many times through out the Scripture as the "Son of Man," because the Law would require a blood relative to *"Redeem"* those who were sold into slavery. Paul, speaking of Jesus as the redeemer, tells us Philippians 2:6-8, *"Who, being in very nature God, did not consider equality with God something to be grasped, but made himself nothing, taking the very nature of a servant, being made in human likeness. And being found in appearance as a man, he humbled himself and became obedient to death -even death on a cross!"* All of this so the believing man could be legally free from the Law of Sin and Death.

You can see at this point that Law is built upon Law. Redemption and the "Law of the Spirit of Life" are not just New Covenant ideas, but are legal concepts found in the Torah that can declare a man free by the Law's fulfillment. Jesus, in Matthew 5:17-18, says that he came to *"fulfill"* the Law and then his statement at the end of verse 18 tells us that not everything is *"accomplished."* While this sounds like a contradiction, it is possible because the Law of Sin and Death (like the Law of the Spirit of Life) is fulfilled one person at a time. Thus, it can be fulfilled AND not yet fully accomplished at the same time.

PAUL ON FAITH AND THE LAW

Every Bible student who has taken on the task of studying the New Testament has faced the complexity of the Apostle Paul. Paul is an expert on both the Law and Grace. He looks at every issue from both perspectives, and we must be careful to hear both perspectives. He is an expert on the Law because of his education and his pedigree and an expert on Grace because of what he had received. Paul identified his Jewishness like this in Philippians 3:5-6: "*...circumcised on the eighth day, of the people of Israel, of the tribe of Benjamin, a Hebrew of Hebrews; in regard to the Law, a Pharisee; as for zeal, persecuting the church; as for legalistic righteousness, faultless.*" Yet when it comes to Grace, Paul will say, in Ephesians 1:7, *"In him we have redemption through his blood, the forgiveness of sins, in accordance with the riches of God's grace. "* It is Paul's experiences with Grace and his background in the Law which makes him the expert on the differences between **keeping** the Law and **relying** on the Law. This difference in keeping the Law as compared to relying on the Law shall be a primary factor in determining the validity of Messianic worship and practice. In fact, this is what is at the heart of the argument that says that the Messianic movement is a return to legalism. The question is: is there a difference in **keeping** the Law and **relying** on the Law?

If the Bible speaks so clearly on faith, and so clearly defines the purpose of the Law, then where has all this historical contention and misunderstanding come from? The problem has been two-fold, stemming from those who want to be justified by Faith without the Law, and from those who want to be justified by the Law without Faith. These two theological camps have existed from the beginning of the time, when God called the Jews to faith. One of the early arguments can be easily traced back to the time of Habakkuk 2:4 where Habakkuk declares that righteousness is measured by faithfulness. For nearly three thousand years, men have been insisting that these two aspects of the early Jewish belief system could, and should, be separated. So, it is no wonder that the ideas are equally prevalent in the church today. Yet the truth of the Scripture, as we will see, is that the two are inseparable and that either one without the other is unscriptural.

<u>Law</u> <u>Without</u> <u>Faith</u>

<u>Galatians</u> <u>3:10-11</u> *<u>All</u> <u>who</u> <u>rely</u> <u>on</u>* observing the Law are under a curse, for it is written: "Cursed is everyone who does not continue to do everything written in the Book of the Law." *<u>Clearly</u> <u>no</u> <u>one</u> <u>is</u> <u>justified</u> <u>before</u> <u>God</u> <u>by</u> <u>the</u> <u>Law,</u> <u>because,</u> <u>"The</u> <u>righteous</u> <u>will</u> <u>live</u> <u>by</u> <u>faith."</u> <u>(NIV)</u>

In this text, the Apostle Paul finds fault with certain Jewish believers, (called Judaizers) not because they are Torah-keepers, but because they *"rely"* on the Law to justify themselves. This, of course, would be contrary to Habakkuk 2:4 *"...but the righteous will live by his faith."* Not only is relying on the Law for justification contrary to the books of Habakkuk and Galatians, but it is also contrary to the very purpose of the Law. As we have already discovered, the Torah was to govern the lives of the Jewish people on a day-to-day basis as well as direct their spiritual worship. Its purpose was to give order and structure to life, as well as definition to sin. Paul correctly reminds them, *"Clearly no one is justified before God by the Law,* because, *The righteous will live by faith."* Later, Paul would also say in II Corinthians 5:21, *"God made him who had no sin to be sin for us, so that in him we might become the righteousness of God."* To *rely* on the Law is to *rely* on one's own ability to keep the law, and to maintain a state of self-righteousness. Once again, the key word here is **RELY,** it is not **OBSERVE.** Paul is speaking only to those Judaizers who would *rely* on the Law.

You may wish to note that even before Jesus' birth, faith was the only means to God, it was never a matter of *relying* on the Law. In the Old Testament, the most common expression or phrase concerning faith is "Trust in the Lord." This phrase appears 15 times in the Old Testament, and "trust in God" another 61 times. I have concluded that when Christians use the term *Faith* they most often mean *Trust,* and when a Jew uses the term *Trust* he often means *Faith.* According to Strong's Concordance the most common Greek word for faith is "peitho" {pi'-tho} which means to "persuade, trust, obey, have confidence, believe." David said, to those who were wavering in their faith, *"Trust in the LORD with all your heart and lean not on your own understanding."* Even though faith that is willing to declare that much trust is rarely seen in today's world, it was not inconceivable even in the time of King David.

Galatians 5:3-5 *Again* **I declare to every man who lets himself be circumcised that he is obligated to obey the whole Law.** *You who are trying to be justified by Law have been alienated from Christ;* **you have fallen away from grace. But by faith we eagerly await through the Spirit the righteousness for which we hope. (NIV)**

And here is yet another warning to those would misuse the Law of Moses, by confusing the purpose for which it was given. The issue in this text, at first, may appear to be circumcision, but it is not. The problem is that there were (and some still are) some believers who wanted to make prerequisites to salvation. Circumcision in itself was not the issue, the issue was the absence of faith and the resulting misuse of the Law.   Paul, when he says, "*...you who are trying to be justified by the Law*" is speaking to that special group of people who we have identified as the "Judaizers." If we learn nothing else from the study of this chapter, we must understand once again what the purpose of the Law was when it was given. The Scriptures tell us, in the New Testament as well as in the Old Testament, that we are justified by Faith, as our father Abraham was. Don't forget that Abraham was found righteous by faith before the Law was ever given. For those who may not be Old Testament historians, Abraham was an Old Testament figure, yet he was found righteous by his faith.

Now, I do have another one of those side notes on circumcision that really does need to come to the surface.

Circumcision was a covenant sign, given by God **BEFORE** the Law of Moses, to Abraham, who is the Father of faith. The sign of circumcision was later included in the Torah covenant, but it did not originate with Moses. The Patriarch Abraham was not under any Law when he was circumcised. Circumcision is the covenant sign that God gave for all the natural born children of Abraham. The covenant sign of circumcision was given to Abraham, who is called the man of faith, and later it was reinforced by the covenant that was given to Moses. One might even say that this reinstatement of the circumcision sign was an infusion of the role of faith into the Law. Again, Abraham's covenant did not end, but was in fact incorporated into this new covenant given to Moses.

Faith Without Law

Romans 3:27-31 Where, then, is boasting? It is excluded. On what principle? On that of observing the Law? No, but on that of _faith_. _For we maintain that a man is justified by faith apart from observing the Law._ Is God the God of Jews only? Is he not the God of Gentiles too? Yes, of Gentiles too, since there is only one God, who will justify the circumcised by faith and the uncircumcised through that same faith. _Do we, then, nullify the Law by this faith? Not at all! Rather, we uphold the Law._ (NIV)

We now come to another critical question that needs to be asked, "Does Faith cancel out the Torah and its Laws?" Or maybe the question should be, "Does it replace the keeping of the Torah and its Law?" Is the Torah and the rest of the Old Testament still supposed to mean something to the Believer in Jesus?

Rather than me trying to answer this question for you, we will let our expert on Law and Grace do it for us. Paul answers the question like this:

<u>Romans</u> <u>3:31</u> **_<u>"Do</u> <u>we,</u> <u>then,</u> <u>nullify</u> <u>the</u> <u>Law</u> <u>by</u> <u>this faith? Not</u> <u>at</u> <u>all!</u> <u>Rather,</u> <u>we</u> <u>uphold</u> <u>the</u> <u>Law.</u>"_**

Though this may be a revelation to some, the fact remains that New Testament teaches that _"Faith"_ is supposed to _"uphold the Law."_ The two are NOT in contradiction to one another. The two are NOT in conflict with each other. Instead, as we see in this text, they are found working in harmony to bring about the salvation of mankind. The issue of "faith verses the Law" is not a Biblical issue, but a man-made issue.

I do realize that there are people who will disagree with my interpretation on the writings of the Apostle Paul. Some may even disagree on my method of using word studies or my line of logic. But there remains one piece of compelling evidence that is undeniable, and that is what the Apostle Paul practiced. While there can be disagreement as to the exact meaning of Paul's writings, there cannot be any confusion about Paul actions and what he did. The measure of Paul's theology may not be fully understood by just studying his writings alone but I do believe it can be understood when seen in conjunction with his worship and that which he practiced. Since the earliest age of the Church, theologians have argued over the meaning of some of Paul's teachings, yet their biggest arena for confusion and argument has been over this portion of Scripture found in Acts 21:17-26. This is the section which reveals Paul keeping the regulations of the Torah well after the crucifixion of Jesus and after the day of Pentecost.

<u>Acts 21:17-26</u> **When we arrived at Jerusalem, the brothers received us warmly. The next day Paul and the rest of us went to see James, and all the elders were present. Paul greeted them and reported in detail what God had done among the Gentiles through his ministry.**

When they heard this, they praised God. Then they said to Paul: "*You see, brother, how many thousands of Jews have believed, and all of them are zealous for the law. They have been informed that you teach all the Jews who live among the Gentiles to turn away from Moses, telling them not to circumcise their children or live according to our customs.* What shall we do? They will certainly hear that you have come, *so do what we tell you. There are four men with us who have made a vow. Take these men, join in their purification rites and pay their expenses, so that they can have their heads shaved. Then everybody will know there is no truth in these reports about you, but that you yourself are living in obedience to the law.* As for the Gentile believers, we have written to them our decision that they should abstain from food sacrificed to idols, from blood, from the meat of strangled animals and from sexual immorality."

The next day Paul took the men and purified himself along with them. Then he went to the temple to give notice

of the date when the days of purification would end and the offering would be made for each of them. (NIV)

This rarely-discussed passage identifies several very interesting points. First, that Paul willingly participated in "purification rites" in the Temple, and secondly, that he willingly "paid the expenses" for these other men to shave their heads and make a sacrifice in the Temple. Most scholars agree that this whole passage refers to some men who were making a Nazarite vow, and were consecrating themselves to the Nazarite way of life. The offering that was required was a sacrifice. That means that Paul was willing to pay for, and participate in, a sacrifice for the sake of a vow. Of course, this all occurred after the death and resurrection of Jesus.

Now, there are only two possible explanations for Paul's actions here. The first is that the Apostle Paul, under pressure, gave in to the wishes of the other Apostles (Peter, James, John, etc.) who apparently did not know and understand the truth of the fulfillment of the Scriptures and the teachings of Jesus. If this is the explanation, then Paul, in his personal weakness, violates his own teachings and thus proves himself to be a spineless hypocrite in the matter of the Law. It would also prove that the other Apostles were not really in tune with the work Jesus had done. Or, there is the second possibility, which is in keeping with the analysis of this book. That is that the Apostle Paul himself was a practicing New Testament Messianic who was liberated by the work of the cross from sin and death **AND** yet continued to live a Torah-observant lifestyle. If this is true, then a Torah lifestyle may still be valid for the believers today. But so there is no confusion, let tell you what I am not saying. I am not saying we should return to the legalistic yokes that our fathers knew. If anyone is trying to rely on the Law to prove something, then they have already gone astray.

However, I suspect that the real issue of faith verses Law came into effect as Christianity became a multi-cultural religion. If we recall, part of the Torah was to establish the believers as a society (culture). The early church began growing by crossing what were previously considered to be taboo cultural lines. As a religion, the church's theology was being assimilated into, and influenced by, those cultures and countries of the Diaspora. This could explain why the religion of Christianity grew and yet the Biblical Jewish Lifestyle was lost. Though people accepted and received the theology, the early churches came into being in pagan cultures with pagan practices. Without the Torah lifestyle, the Old Testament would appear to be nothing more than legalism to the reader. However, it is not the purpose of this study to evaluate the historical evidence and issues that arose as the church became more and more Romanized.

With the ministry of the Apostle Paul breaking forth on the scene, the real question of the early church was, "What do we do with the Gentiles and the Torah?" Two thousand years later, the question has now become reversed: "What do we do with the Messianic and the Torah?"

FAITH AND THE PROMISES OF ABRAHAM

Romans 4:13-16   *It was not through Law* that Abraham and his offspring received the promise that he would be heir of the world, but through the *righteousness that comes by faith*. For if those who live by Law are heirs, faith has no value and the promise is worthless, because Law brings wrath. And where there is no Law there is no transgression. *Therefore, the promise comes by faith, so that it may be by grace* and may be guaranteed to all Abraham's offspring - not only to those who are of the Law but also to those who are of the faith of Abraham. He is the father of us all. (NIV)

Paul, the writer of Romans, helps us to understand that there is a Covenant that is older than the Law of Moses (Torah). In fact, the Law was given in order to bring the people to the *"Fulfillment"* of that older Covenant and its promises which had been given to Abraham. It was not through the Law that Abraham received the promises of God, for Abraham lived hundreds of years before the Torah was given. It was through his Faith in the Promise-Giver that he received the first installment of what would be the lasting Covenants. Paul does well when he says, *"Therefore, the promise comes by faith, so that it may be by grace....not only to those who are of the Law but also to those who are of the faith of Abraham. He is the father of us all."* All you have to understand is, what is this *"faith of*

Abraham"? The answer can found in the study Hebrews 11:8-19. This is where we find the list of the acts and deeds of Abraham's faith, as recounted by the Apostle Paul. But for the sake of time, let us examine Romans 4:3 and discover just what Abraham did that was so pleasing to the Lord.

<u>**Romans 4:3**</u> **What does the Scripture say? "Abraham *believed* *God*, and it was credited to him as righteousness." (NIV)**

BELIEVED

4100 pisteuo {pist-yoo'-o} from 4102;
AV - believe 239, commit unto 4, commit to (one's) trust 1, be committed unto 1, be put in trust with 1, be commit to one's trust 1, believer 1;
1) to think to be true, be persuaded of, to credit, place confidence in
1a) of the thing believed
1a1) to credit, have confidence
2) to entrust a thing to one, i.e. his fidelity
2a) to be entrusted with a thing

I know this may appear too simple for some people to grasp, but all that Abraham really did was *"believe God"* and act accordingly. To be like Abraham is what the Lord still desires and requires from His people, and that is to simply believe God. We must remember that all who believe, both Jew and Gentile alike, and that have Faith in Y'shua the Messiah, are the children of Abraham, and have become heirs to the promises. Sadly, most Christians do not know what those promises are, since they come from the Old Testament.

Please allow me at this time to give you another item of food for thought. If the Old Testament has "passed away," as some Christians believe, then did the promises that it held for **ALL** of Abraham's children also pass away? If so, then to what do we, as believers, look for? In what have we become joint heirs?

Of course, there is the teaching of Replacement Theology, which says the promises that God gave to Abraham did not pass away, He just took them away from Abraham's children, and gave them to someone else.

<u>Romans 5:1-2</u>   Therefore, since we have been _justified through faith_, we have peace with God through our Lord Jesus Christ, through whom we have gained access _by faith into this grace in which we now stand._ And we rejoice in the hope of the glory of God. (NIV)

There are two elements in Romans 5:1-2 that we need to identify if we are ever to understand what it means to be in right relationship with God. First is that _"faith"_ is an act on our part which shows we _"trust"_ in the Lord. The second is that God's _"grace"_ is His act of unmerited favor upon all who have found themselves in opposition to the righteous Law of God, and who seek to be restored. The Scripture which says, _"...all have sinned and come short of the glory of God,"_ (Romans 3:23) implies that both Jew and Gentile are in need of such _"grace."_ In fact, without it, we are left facing a just Law as unjust sinners. It is in this that we know that Jew and Gentile are truly equal.

THE EARLY CHURCH:
JEW AND GENTILE?

With the growing interest in the Messianic movement, some have sought to answer the questions posed to the Gentile Church about the Law by distinguishing a difference between Jewish believers and Gentile believers. Some have gone so far as to teach that there are two sets of plans and standards for salvation, one for the Jews and another for the Gentiles. This is most often referred to as "Dual Covenant Theology." Though there may be some evidence to the fact that there is, or at least was, in Biblical times, a distinction between the two based on culture, the distinction between Jew and Gentile does not and cannot exist on a spiritual level. This is especially crucial if we are talking about the plan or standards for salvation. Much of this misunderstanding comes from Paul's statement which says: "First to the Jew and then to the Gentile."

I must confess that, on the surface, there appears to be some basis for this viewpoint of cultural or racial distinction if one looks at just a few Scriptures, yet there is not enough information to sway me to believe that there is a cultural or racial distinction IN CHRIST between the Jewish and the Gentile believers. The danger of such thoughts leads us to a very critical area of concern, that concern is for a "spiritual class system" in which one of the two, the Jewish or the Gentile believer, becomes a lesser citizen of the Kingdom than the other. Some Scriptures that are used to support such a supposed distinction contain a misunderstood Pauline phrase that is found three times in the book of Romans.

Romans 1:16 I am not ashamed of the gospel, because it is the power of God for the salvation of everyone who believes: *first for the Jew, then for the Gentile. (NIV)*

Romans 2:9-11 There will be trouble and distress for every human being who does evil: *first for the Jew, then for the Gentile*; but glory, honor and peace for everyone who does good: *first for the Jew, then for the Gentile*. For God does not show favoritism. *(NIV)*

FIRST

4412 proton {pro'-ton}First
1) first in time or place
1a) in any succession of things or persons
2) first in rank , influence, honor, chief, principal
3) first, at the first

As we study the Greek word for *"First"* we find that the word really does mean just that, *"First."* However, it does not distinguish a **difference** in quality between Jew and Gentile, as in some kind of class system, it merely **sets an order**. The misunderstanding of this word has fostered the mistaken belief that God deals with the Jews differently than He deals with Gentile believers. This gives the false impression that He has created two *classes* of believers. As Paul clearly points out, in Galatians *3:28 "There is neither Jew nor Greek...in Christ Jesus."* There is no justified

72

"class" system of believers. This Scripture just identifies the order, in time, that these the two people groups would experience trouble and distress and peace and honor, and that the Jews received the Good News first. I also see in this phrase a balancing out, because in the same order the Jew will receive first *"trouble and distress,"* then *"glory, honor and peace."* Once again, in Paul's own words, let us examine this issue of distinction between Jews and Gentiles that believe.

Ephesians 6:9 And masters, treat your slaves in the same way. Do not threaten them, since you know that he who is both their Master and yours is in heaven, and _there is no favoritism with him._ (NIV)

Today, there are real questions with this distinction issue between Jews and Gentiles in Messianic and Traditional congregations on a Biblical and cultural level. If there is a cultural or racial issue, then is the Messianic form of worship a valid form of worship for any one who is not Jewish? If the answer is no, then is Messianic worship just a method of cross-cultural evangelism?

Let us attempt understand the basis for any Biblical or cultural or racial distinction that may exist between Messianic congregations and the Traditional church.

Acts 15:22-29 Then the apostles and elders, with the whole church, decided to choose some of their own men and send them to Antioch with Paul and Barnabas. They chose Judas (called Barnabas) and Silas, two men who were leaders among the brothers.

With them they sent the following letter: The apostles and elders, your brothers, To the Gentile believers in Antioch, Syria and Cilicia: Greetings. We have heard that some went out from us without our authorization and disturbed you, troubling your minds by what they said, So we all agreed to choose some men and send them to you with our dear friends Barnabas and Paul - men who have risked their lives for the name of our Lord Jesus Christ. Therefore we are sending Judas and Silas to confirm by word of mouth what we are writing. _It seemed good to the Holy Spirit and to us not to burden you with anything beyond the following requirements: You are to abstain from food sacrificed to idols, from blood, from the meat of strangled animals and from sexual immorality. You will do well to avoid these things. Farewell._

This Scripture in the book of Acts is far more complicated than it first appears, because of its origin. Acts 15 was written in response to Judaizers who sought to bring the Gentile portion of the church under the whole Law, and to keep portions of the Law that Jesus had already _"fulfilled."_ In essence, the idea was to bring them to a place of _"relying"_ on the Law to prove a state of rightness (which the Law was never meant to do any way). This text in Acts is the Apostles' response to the Judaizers.

In Acts, Chapter 15, we have the four requirements מִצְוֹת (mitzvot or commandments) that were given to the Gentile portion of the church by the Apostles. The question that so few scholars seem to ask is, where did these _"requirements"_ come from and what is their origin? Were they created by necessity, or were they made up by the Apostles? And what was it that made these rules so special as to be given to the Gentile believers?

Here is a little known truth in the matter of these *"requirements."* The requirements found here in the book of Acts for the Gentile believers had already been around for hundreds of years as part of the "Oral tradition" of Judaism. These mitzvots (commandments) would later become part of the Babylonian Talmud for the governing of Jewish and Gentile relationships. These particular four requirements would be joined by three others in 450 CE, and would be referred to as the "Noahide Laws." The Noahide Laws are the rules that governed the actions of righteous Gentiles (ger-tzedeq) and resident Gentiles (ger-toshab) who wished to live with and among the Jews. The Gerim-tzedeqim would later be called "God-Fearers." One such noted "God-Fearer" was Cornelius, who is identified in the book of Acts, Chapter ten. Cornelius' claim to fame is that he was the first Gentile Messianic believer.

<u>Acts 10:1-2</u> At Caesurae there was a man named Cornelius, a centurion in what was known as the Italian Regiment. He and all his family were <u>*devout*</u> <u>*and*</u> <u>*God-fearing;*</u> he gave generously to those in need and prayed to God regularly. (NIV)

In the time of Jesus, God-Fearers were Gentiles who worshipped the God of Israel (although they were limited in what they were permitted to do). They studied the Torah, paid tithes and could later become proselytes to the Jewish faith. The Noahide Laws set the Gentile believers apart from the rest of the pagan world. Their name.. גֵּר *"Ger"* (alien among you)! צֶדֶיק *"tzedeq"* (righteous), was not given lightly, as the new believers had to show an abandonment of their pagan lifestyle. Upon proof of this, they would go through the process called a *"Mikvah"* in Hebrew and *"baptizemo"* in Greek, which we call in English a *"baptism."* (As one of those wonderful side notes, baptism was a common practice long before John the Baptist, going all the way back to the Torah and Moses.) A ger-toshab is one who lived among the Jews and maybe was even a worshiper of the God of Israel, but he is best seen understood as a quasi-citizen in the Jewish community. In either case, the whole of the Law was not placed upon a Gentile living in the midst of the Jewish community unless he/she became a proselyte. The Noahide Laws governed the lives of these Gentiles who wished to live among, and yet not fully become, Jews.

With the increasing number of Gentiles that wish to join the early Messianic movement, the Apostles, lead by the Holy Spirit, drew from oral traditions (which would later become the Talmud) a set of standards by which the righteous (that is, believing) Gentiles could live. This standard, while not imposing the full weight of the Torah on them, would still require that they no longer lives as pagans and aliens. The "Mikvah" was to become the outward sign of their inward change. It would also stand as the testimony of a changed life that both Jew and Gentile would share in Christ.

These Noahide Laws were the Laws that governed the lives of the righteous Gentiles, those who chose to identify with the theology of New Testament Judaism. This New Testament Judaic theology is still the basis of Christianity.

So we must now return to our original question of "Is there a distinction between Jewish and Gentile believers in Christ?" For the answer, let us turn our minds to the words of the Apostle Paul in Romans and Galatians.

<u>Galatians</u> <u>3:26-28</u> You are all sons of God through faith in Christ Jesus, for all of you who were baptized into Christ have clothed yourselves with Christ. *<u>There</u> <u>is</u> <u>neither</u> <u>Jew</u> <u>nor</u> <u>Greek</u>, <u>slave</u> <u>nor</u> <u>free</u>, <u>male</u> <u>nor</u> <u>female</u>, <u>for</u> <u>you</u> <u>are</u> <u>all</u> <u>one</u> <u>in</u> <u>Christ</u> <u>Jesus.</u>* (NIV)

<u>Romans</u> <u>10:12</u> For *<u>there</u> <u>is</u> <u>no</u> <u>difference</u> <u>between</u> <u>Jew</u> <u>and</u> <u>Gentile</u>* - the same Lord is Lord of all and richly blesses all who call on him, (NIV)

In Acts 15 we see that there appears to be one set of Laws for the Jewish believers, another for the Gentile believers. Then we later read that Paul says that there is no distinction between Jews and Gentiles in Romans and Galatians. So how do we justify these two sets of Scriptures? Let us remember that both Scriptures say "...*in Christ Jesus.*" This is a qualifying statement, which refers to the fact that there are no second class citizens in Christ Jesus. The question again arises, "Was there a distinction in the church?" The only answer is "NO." The Gentile believers were grafted into the existing system of faith and its body of believers. That is why, as we study the New Testament and church history, we see that there was no difference in the status of believers. However, there apparently were differences in the *lifestyles* of the early Jewish believers and their Gentile counterparts. This difference in lifestyle is where the two cultures clashed. The Noahide Laws, found in Acts 15, were considered to be the first steps for a new Gentile believer, who would later be adopted into the (Messianic) Jewish community as a proselyte. As proselytes, these believers and their families would no longer be considered to be "Gentiles," but (Messianic) Jews. It is important to note that the first "Christian" congregations were really mixed groups of Messianic Jews and Gentiles converts who maintained synagogue-style worship.

However, we know a division later arose, a division that split the Jewish and Gentile believers, and from which the church would never recover. With the rise of the popularity of Christianity among the Gentiles in the Roman Empire under Constantine, and the resulting paganization of the church, much of the Jewish teaching and influence was stamped out (literally by force) or replaced with pagan practices. Some of the first teachings that were to be lost were the standards referred to as the Noahide Laws.

Each of the New Testament Epistles were written to a mixed congregation that was outside the boundaries of the land of Israel. In fact, the only time that the Apostle Paul ever spoke to a strictly Gentile audience was on Mars Hill in Athens (Acts 17) and it was there that he had zero success in convicting anyone of the truth. History reveals that synagogue-style worship was the practice of the Messianic congregations up till about 280 CE, and that most pre-Constantine Gentile congregations kept many of the traditions of their Jewish counterparts, including celebrating the Feasts of God, the Mikvah (baptism) and Shabbat (Saturday Worship). Christianity was not seen as a separate **religion** from Judaism until the Constantine Revolution. With the paganization of the church and the introduction of Christian idolatry (i.e. the veneration of saints, the elevation of Mary, etc.) the last of the Jewish influence would be removed and a great barrier would be put in its place. Today, in orthodox Jewish synagogues and, as of late, in a few Messianic synagogues in Israel, Gentiles may still participate as God-Fearers (Ger-tzedeq). The same rules for participation still apply, for the most part, to any Gentile who wishes to live in Israel. Though not forced by the Law of the land, they are surely pushed by the social pressure to conform. As far as the church is concerned, I do not know of any Gentile congregation or church (except possibly the Seventh Day Adventists) that keeps the Noahide Laws as a practice/doctrine.

KEEPING THE CUSTOMS AND PRACTICES

So, shall we ask another one of those questions that is at the heart of our study? "Should a **Christian** keep the Laws of the Torah or the Jewish customs (except for the portions that are/were fulfilled by Messiah)?"

Colossians 2:13-17   **When you were dead in your sins and in the uncircumcision of your sinful nature, God made you alive with Christ.** _He forgave us all our sins, having canceled the written code, with its regulations, that was against us and that stood opposed to us;_ **(the Law of sin and death) he took it away, nailing it to the cross. And having disarmed the powers and authorities, he made a public spectacle of them, triumphing over them by the cross.** _Therefore do not let anyone judge you_ **by what you eat or drink, or with regard to a religious festival, a New Moon celebration or a Sabbath day.** _These are a shadow of the things that were to come; the reality, however, is found in Christ._ _(NIV)_

Paul writes to the Colossian congregation, which, like all the congregations of Paul's ministry, is a mixed congregation of Jews and Gentiles, and he reminds them that Jesus has "_canceled_" the charges made against them under the Law. Some Christians actually believe that the Torah and its statutes were nailed to the cross and not our sin charges. It was not the Torah, but Jesus, as our substitutional sacrifice, who was nailed to the cross. If it was the Torah, then the Law would truly have ended, since the cross is an instrument of death and destruction. The canceling of our sins took place by His *"fulfilling"* of the Law. As it says in II Corinthians 5:21, *"God made him who had no sin to be sin for us"* so we could become the Righteousness of God. Paul then speaks of the freedom of the believer concerning the Torah practices and customs. Here, he neither condemns nor supports these practices, but suggests that the believer has a freedom from being judged by others (Judaizers) who would condemn. We should understand that there is a freedom to keep, or not to keep, the customs and practices surrounding the Law. This by no means gives us liberty to sin at will, or to ignore the Word of God, for it is still the Law, in the hands of the Holy Spirit, that convicts us of sin. Many Christians today cannot understand why anyone would volunteer to keep such customs and practices, and find it easier to chalk it all up to legalism rather than to seek understanding. Yet often times, the very same people will keep Thanksgiving or the Fourth of July, which are just national holidays, with all that modern tradition dictates in the form of turkey and fireworks. This is not to imply that doing such things are wrong, but to ask, why keep the feasts of men and ignore the Biblically appointed times of God?

The value of keeping such Biblical practices as Passover (Peasha) or Rosh Hashanah (Feast of Trumpets, also the Biblical New Year) may be best understood in Paul last statement in Colossians 2:17 *"These are a shadow of the things that were to come; the reality, however, is found in Christ."* As shadows, they are meant to be teaching devices that will reveal truth and insight about Jesus as Messiah to the student of the Scriptures. It is also true that those who keep these practices believe that they are Biblically, if not legalistically, required. Later on, in his letter to the Galatians, Paul deals with the Judaizers who were not content with this freedom of choice in the expression of spiritual practices. These Judaizers not only wished to see the Messianic Jewish community, but also the Gentile portion of the church, keeping their (Judaizers') customs and practices. In so doing, they desired to make these practices a type of legalistic requirement, if not for conversion, at least as some type of spiritual maintenance program.

Galatians 2:14 When I saw that they were not acting in line with the truth of the gospel, I said to Peter in front of them all, "You are a Jew, yet you live like a Gentile and not like a Jew. _How is it, then, that you force Gentiles to follow Jewish customs?"_ (NIV)

FORCE

anagkazo {an-ang-kad'-zo} AV - compel, constrain
1) to necessitate, compel, drive to, constrain
1a) by force, threats, etc.
1b) by permission, entreaties,
1c) by other means

Paul's complaint was not that the Messianics and Gentiles were keeping the Jewish customs, but that they were keeping the customs **because of the pressure** that was brought to bear on them. The freedom to keep or not to keep had already been established and made clear. The issue here is *force*. It was the desire of the Judaizers to control the Messainics and their new found freedom in Messiah.

It is my opinion that this is a lesson that the modern church, like the historical Jewish community, has not learned. Church history is replete with time periods and events during which oppressive cultural forces (in the name of the church) were applied, as well as times when physical violence, under the guise of religion, was used to bring other (especially non-Christian) cultures into conformity. Among these shameful acts of history we have the Spanish Inquisition, the ethnic cleansing of the Holocaust, and the story of the early mission work in the Hawaiian Islands, just to name a few. Then there are the Crusades, which amount to simple murder, rape and plundering in the name of God and His Christ. If anything could be said of historical Christendom, it can be said that we have truly outdone our Jewish ancestors when it comes to *force*.

In reference to our original question, the only Biblical conclusion is that Christians and Messianics may rejoice and celebrate the Biblical Feasts and the practices of our Jewish history as long as the celebration and practice is not forced, and as long as it does not represent itself as a prerequisite for salvation, or as mandatory for maintenance of one's righteousness.

COVENANT REPLACEMENT THEOLOGY

The teaching of the doctrine centering around the *New Covenant* is the very foundation on which the church stands. And yet the idea of the New Covenant has also been misinterpreted to generate one of the largest theological errors of all time, which is tantamount to theological and Biblical suicide. This error is known as the doctrine of Replacement Theology. Covenant Replacement Theology is one of the mistakes of Third Century Christendom to which many denominations still hold. This teaching seeks to establish the misconception that the Jews of Jesus' and Paul's time had completely rejected the Messiah and thus God's Covenant relationship with Israel, and that as a result of that rejection, God "replaced" the Jews with the Church in all of His Covenants and promises. The historical facts are that some scholars believe that as much as a fourth of all First Century Jews believed that Jesus was the Messiah of God's people, Israel. A simple examination of Acts, chapter 21, where the Apostles are speaking to Paul, will help us to understand the reality of the actual numbers, *"Look how many thousands believe."* This shows us that there was not the wholesale rejection by the Jews that as some would believe. Some of the early replacement teachers who help to promote such misconceptions were Chrysostom, Hippolytus and Origen.

In the fourth century, Chrysostom, a very well know teacher of his day, said of the Jews:

"How can a Christian dare have the slightest converse with a Jew, most miserable of all men?"

"The rejection and dispersion of the Jews was the work of God not the emperors. It was done by the wrath of God and His absolute abandon of you."

"It is the duty of Christians to hate the Jews: he who can never love Christ enough will never have done fighting against those Jews who hate Him."

With this supposed rejection, all the Biblical promises and prophecies concerning Israel were to have shifted from the Jews to the Gentiles, and the Biblical covenants (Old and New Testament) now belong exclusively to the established Gentile New-Testament-Only Church. This teaching of Replacement Theology has gone to such extremes that some denominations have actually required that any Jewish person who wished to be a "Christian Convert" had to totally denounce his/her Jewish heritage. For instance, not only was this a common practice among early churches but Lutherans and Catholics actually sought to document the legitimacy of the individual's conversion by having the supposed converts eat pork or perform some other practice that was in violation of the Law (Torah). If one did not wish to convert to Christianity, there were always the evangelism techniques of the Inquisition. The European Rabbis of the Middle Ages knew that many of the Jews had to "convert" in order to save their lives or the lives of their families. It is because of this *forced evangelism* that the prayer said on Yom Kippur, the *Kol Nidre,* came into bring. The Kol Nidre seeks forgiveness and release from a vow that was made under duress, one that would not, or could not, be kept.

This Third Century error, the idea that God has rejected Israel, was one of the first and one of the most destructive errors that Christians have come to believe. We know that this is incorrect for several reasons. First, because to do so would be contrary to God's very nature. Of course, we are aware, of times past when He withdrew His presence for a season, so that Israel might learn some valuable lesson. Yet each time, after such lessons, the Lord returned His presence to a newly-revived Israel. In similar ways, He returns His presence to a returning backslider today. In Jewish thought, such a person is called a *"Ta'shuv'ah"* or a returnee.

A *tashuvah* is one who has returned, as even from the dead. God's promises of never abandoning His people are found throughout the Scriptures, in both New and Old Testament. Deut. 4:31 *says "For the Lord your God is a merciful God; he will not abandon or destroy you or forget the covenant with your fathers, which he confirmed to them by oath. "* Then in the New Testament, it says in Romans 11:29 *"...for God's gifts and his call are irrevocable. "* There are many Old Testament Scriptures that tell us the same message over and over again. It is this very concept that we, as individuals, count on, and call Grace. As it was the nature of the father, in the parable of the Prodigal Son, to look for his son's return, so it is God's nature to not abandon His people.

Secondly, there are also the teachings of Paul on this matter:

Romans 11:1-2 *I ask then: Did God reject his people? By no means!* I am an Israelite myself, a descendant of Abraham, from the tribe of Benjamin. *God did not reject his people, whom he foreknew.* (NIV)

Romans 11:11-12 Again I ask: *Did they stumble so as to fall beyond recovery? Not at all!* Rather, because of their transgression, salvation has come to the Gentiles to make Israel envious. But if their transgression means riches for the world, and their loss means riches for the Gentiles, how much greater riches will their fullness bring! (NIV)

As stated earlier, many historians believe that as much as twenty-five percent of all Israel became believers in Jesus as the Messiah. The Apostles, in Acts chapter 21, said to Paul *"You see, brother, how many thousands of Jews have believed, and all of them are zealous for the Law?"* At best, one could say that a portion of Jews did reject Jesus as the Messiah, and that those natural branches, according to the book of Romans, were removed. However, the reason for their removal was their unbelief, not because they were Jews. If we continue speaking in the same symbolic terms as Paul, removing some of the branches does not mean that the whole tree was cut down! The Scripture also does not say, as many may think, that the Gentiles (who were converts to Messianic Judaism) were grafted into the removed branches' sockets or into the place from which the unbelieving had been taken. This would be silly, to graft a good branch into a socket that had been despised. What it does say is that they (the Gentile Messianic believers) *"...have been grafted in among the others."* The others, of course, being the believing Messianic Jewish community that remained intact, as did the original tree. The grafting in of the Gentiles could not, and should not, have taken place if the whole tree was diseased or invalid.

Romans 11:17-18   If some of the branches have been broken off, and you, though a wild olive shoot, _have been grafted in among the others_ and now share in the nourishing sap from the olive root, do not boast over those branches. If you do, _consider this: You do not support the root, but the root supports you._ _(NIV)_

Those who are of the school of Replacement Theology have a problem with any Scripture that mentions Israel by name. In order to justify their view that the "New Testament Only" Gentile church has replaced Israel, the replacement theologists attempt to see themselves as some sort of _spiritual Israel or as spiritualized Jews_, rather than as the adopted children they were meant to be. _Spiritual Jewishness_ is another vague, nebulous concept, with no definition. It lacks any type of Biblical validation. In essence, it is supposed to somehow imply that the Gentiles are _New Jews or Real Jews_, with all the rights to the Biblical promises of Abraham and to his descendants, while being able to live as Gentiles (i.e. outside of the Law).

I sometimes stand in wonder at the logic of Replacement Theology and I have had to ask myself a number of questions in trying to understand their position. Does God really get so mad as to break His own word and withdraw His promises? And, if so, if He did it once, will He do it again? Can God be trusted? Is the promise of our salvation a sure promise? Of course, you and I both know that it is ridiculous for me to think such things and ask such questions, for God is faithful and true, and His word will stand forever. And yet, this is the basis, the very foundation and logic of those who would promote Replacement Theology. That is, those who choose to call themselves "Spiritual Israel," rather than adopted or grafted-in children.

<u>Romans</u> <u>11:17</u>   ... and you though a wild olive shoot, have been grafted in among the others and now share in the nourishing sap from the olive root, (NIV)

JESUS AND THE NEW COVENANT

While studying the *New Covenant*, we will expose several of the flaws found in Replacement Theology, as well study as the differences, similarities and the purposes of the New and Old Covenants. Let us start by examining the two most revealing and pivotal chapters in the New Testament on this subject, Hebrews 8 and 9. It might be well for the reader, at this time, to read these chapters in Hebrews in their entirety before continuing here.

Hebrews 8:6-13 But the ministry *Jesus has received is as superior to theirs as the covenant of which he is mediator is superior to the old one,* and it is founded on better promises. *For if there had been nothing wrong with that first covenant, no place would have been sought for another.* But God found fault with the people and said: "The time is coming, declares the Lord, when *I will make a new covenant with the house of Israel and with the house of Judah. It will not be like the covenant I made with their forefathers* when I took them by the hand to lead them out of Egypt, because they did not remain faithful to my covenant, and I turned away from them, declares the Lord. *This is the covenant I will make with the house of Israel* after that time, declares the Lord. I will put my Laws in their minds and write them on their hearts. I will be their God, and they will be my people. No longer will a man teach his neighbor, or a man his brother, saying, `Know the Lord,' because they will all know me, from the least of them to the greatest.*

For I will forgive their wickedness and will remember their sins no more." By calling this covenant "new," he has made the first one obsolete; and what is obsolete and aging will soon disappear. (NIV)

Here, in Hebrews, Chapter 8, we find a promise quoted from Jeremiah 31:13-34, that the Lord God would make a New Covenant with his people, not because He had found fault with the first covenant, but had *"...found fault with the people, and said: The time is coming, declares the Lord, when I will make a new covenant."* His New Covenant would be greater than the first because it would be *"founded on better promises."* For those who may not have noticed, the book of Jeremiah is not found in the New Testament. The first mention of the New Covenant happens to be found in the Old Testament. This text in Hebrews goes on to describe some of the concepts and criteria of the New Covenant:

Hebrews 8:10-12   This is the covenant I will make with the house of Israel after that time, declares the Lord. *I will put my Laws in their minds and write them on their hearts. I will be their God, and they will be my people. No longer will a man teach his neighbor, or a man his brother, saying, "Know the Lord," because they will all know me, from the least of them to the greatest. For I will forgive their wickedness and will remember their sins no more. (NIV)*

These clearly are the terms of the New Testament Covenant and yet, in spite of the beliefs of those who believe in Replacement Theology, one can't help but noticing that this is a covenant made with the *House of Israel.* In fact, if you study the Scriptures in the New and Old Testament, you will find that God has never made a covenant with Gentiles. He has always maintained the plan of their inclusion into the existing covenant, yet there has never been an independent covenant made for or with them. As Christians, we believe that the New Covenant was instituted with the death and the resurrection of Jesus Christ. In this New Covenant, sealed by His death, only the *House of Israel* is named by name. At the time of the death of the one who writes a will or covenant, that document can no longer be altered. (Hebrews 9:16)

I am not saying this to disposes the Gentile believers, but to ask the question, where do the Gentile Believers come in? With a little help from the Book of Romans, we will see again how the Gentiles fit into this New Covenant.

<u>Romans 11:13-21</u> *<u>I am talking to you Gentiles</u>*. **Inasmuch as I am the apostle to the Gentiles, I make much of my ministry in the hope that I may some how arouse my own people to envy and save some of them. For if their rejection is the reconciliation of the world, what will their acceptance be but life from the dead? If the part of the dough offered as firstfruits is holy, then the whole batch is holy; if the root is holy, so are the branches. If <u>some</u> of the branches have been broken off, and you, though a wild olive shoot, <u>have been grafted</u> in among the others and now share in the nourishing sap from the olive root, do not boast over those branches. If you do, consider this: <u>You do not support the root, but the</u>**

92

root supports you. You will say then, "Branches were broken off so that I could be grafted in." Granted. but they were broken off because of unbelief, and you stand by faith. Do not be arrogant, but be afraid. **For if God did not spare the natural branches, he will not spare you either. (NIV)**

The Gentiles (ger-tzedeq) who have become fellow believers in Christ with the Jewish believers (Messianic) are the grafted-in branches spoken of here. The trunk and the nourishment of the root comes from Biblical Jewish Israel. Not just Jewish Israel, but **Biblical,** Jewish Israel. It was to Biblical, Jewish Israel, and to the grafted-in branches of the Gentiles, that the New Covenant was given. Without Biblical Israel, the Gentiles have nothing into which they can be grafted, and thus no hope of participation in this New Covenant.

Hebrews 9:15 For this reason _Christ is the mediator of a new covenant,_ that those who are called may receive the promised eternal inheritance - now that he has died as a ransom _to set them free from the sins committed under the first covenant._

COVENANT

1242 diatheke {dee-ath-ay'-kay} from 1303;
1) a disposition, arrangement, of any sort, which one wishes to   be valid, the last disposition which one makes of his earthly possessions after his death, a testament or will
2) a compact, a covenant, a testament
2a) God's covenant with Noah, etc.

Have you ever noticed or wondered about the legal terms found in the New Testament Scriptures, terms such as justified, or justification, judge or judgment? These terms paint a picture of a courtroom setting. Some Scriptures refer to Satan as the Adversary (in Greek, that is a "prosecutor") and Jesus is referred to as our Advocate. Even the term "covenant" means a legally binding agreement. God's love has insured our salvation, even from the legal perspective, so that no one may challenge our right to His Kingdom. A study on the Old Testament Laws of Redemption would reveal the legal rights of Jesus, as the Son of Man, to redeem mankind. One such Law that we have already looked at is Leviticus 25:48-49 "*....he retains the right of redemption after he has sold himself*" and then "*....one of his relatives may redeem him.*" An uncle or a cousin or any blood relative in his clan may redeem him.

Let there be no misunderstanding or doubt in the reader's mind that Christ is the *"Mediator"* of the *"New Covenant,"* upon which the church is built. This Covenant is the very foundation and the only means of and to legal salvation. The questions we now asking are, what are the terms of this binding legal document we call the "New Covenant," and how does it differ from the "Old Covenant," and what relationship, if any, do the two have with each other?

The word for covenant in Greek is *diatheke*, which best describes a legal will and testament, a document which is unchangeable and binding **after** the death of the party that created it. The bodily, natural death of Jesus sealed His covenant, and made it unchangeable and binding. This was the same covenant that He spoke of and described in the last Passover which He shared with His disciples, when He said:

Luke 22:17-20   After taking the cup, he gave thanks and said, "Take this and divide it among you. For I tell you I will not drink again of the fruit of the vine until the kingdom of God comes." And he took bread, gave thanks and broke it, and gave it to them, saying, "This is my body given for you; do this in remembrance of me." in the same way, after the supper he took the cup, saying, _"This cup is the new covenant in my blood, which is poured out for you."_ (NIV)

It is no accident that Jesus makes this declaration concerning the New Covenant during the Passover, or that the declaration takes place in the middle of the symbols of the Passover, which is one of Judaism's most sacred events. The Passover Feast is the commemoration of the liberation of the Jews from their bondage in Egypt. Here, the Lord uses the Passover to declare the liberation of the believers, but this time, it is the liberation from the Law of Sin and Death. This single event (Passover) is the common instrument that God has used to declare both his First and his Second Covenants to the world. In both New and Old Testament, the Passover was the forerunner to the soon-coming Liberating covenants. Some of today's leading Eschatology (end times) scholars believe that the Rapture/Second Coming of Messiah shall be in accordance with the time of Passover. Even in light of these most important Biblical events, many Christian believers still do not know that the Lords Supper is really a portion of the

Passover ceremony. They are also not aware that the keeping of the Passover unto the Lord is to be maintained forever. The New International Version of the Bible says that it is a *"lasting ordinance."* However, the King James has one of its rare moments of clarity here: Exodus 12:14 *"...And this day shall be unto you for a memorial; and ye shall keep it a feast to the LORD throughout your generations; ye shall keep it a feast by an ordinance forever."* Even the American Standard Version combines the two thoughts together with: *"....ye shall keep it a feast by an ordinance for ever."*

The question still remains, what are the similarities and differences in the two covenants? To find the answer, we will need to look at Hebrews, Chapter 9, where the two covenants are laid out, side by side.

Hebrews 9:1-10 is a description of the Old Covenant that the Jews of Paul's time would have understood. In these brief few verses, Paul touches on the Law and the traditions in reference to operation of the Temple, and things that are Holy to every Jew. In a nutshell, he is discussing the very heart of Biblical Jewish faith:

<u>Hebrews 9:1-10</u> Now the first covenant had *<u>regulations for worship</u>* and also *<u>an earthly sanctuary</u>*. A tabernacle was set up. In its first room were the lampstand, *<u>the table and the consecrated bread; this was called the Holy Place</u>*. Behind the second curtain was a room *<u>called the Most Holy Place</u>*, which had the *<u>golden altar of incense and the gold-covered ark of the covenant</u>*. This ark contained the *<u>gold jar of manna, Aaron's staff</u>*

that had budded, and the stone tablets of the covenant. Above the ark were the cherubim of the Glory, overshadowing the atonement cover. But we cannot discuss these things in detail now. When everything had been arranged like this, the priests entered regularly into the outer room to carry on their ministry. But only the high priest entered the inner room, and that only once a year, and never without blood, which he offered for himself and for the sins the people had committed in ignorance. The Holy Spirit was showing by this that the way into the Most Holy Place had not yet been disclosed as long as the First tabernacle was still standing. _This is an illustration for the present time, indicating that the gifts and sacrifices being offered were not able to clear the conscience of the worshiper. They are only a matter of food and drink and various ceremonial washings -- external regulations applying until the time of the new order._ (NIV)

Paul tells us that the First Covenant system and sacrifices are only illustrations for the present time, until the time of the _"new order,"_ Yet, it is understood that it was under the First Covenant system that Jesus would come to offer his life as a sacrifice that could and would _"clear the conscience of the worshiper."_

Hebrews 9:1 Now the first covenant had regulations for worship and also _an earthly sanctuary._ _(NIV)_

The first key to understanding the Covenants is knowing their physical locations and origins. The second factor in understanding is knowing where the blueprint for the construction of the First Covenant originated. In Hebrews Chapter 9:11-14, Paul describes the New Covenant with much the same settings and trappings as the old, but with several very significant differences. Those differences are found in the same question that we asked about the First Covenant, what is its location and origin. The Second Covenant was made in the **TRUE** Tabernacle, before the **TRUE** Ark, and the blood that was offered was not that of sheep and goats, but of the spotless Lamb of God.

Hebrews 9:11-14 When Christ came as high priest of the good things that are already here, he went through _the greater and more perfect tabernacle that is not man-made, that is to say, not a part of this creation_. He did not enter by means of the blood of goats and calves; but he entered the Most Holy Place once for all by his own blood, having obtained eternal redemption. The blood of goats and bulls and the ashes of a heifer sprinkled on those who are ceremonially unclean sanctify them so that they are outwardly clean. _How much more, then, will the blood of Christ, who through the eternal Spirit offered himself unblemished to God, cleanse our consciences from acts that lead to death, so that we may serve the living God! (NIV)_

Hebrews 9:23-25 _It was necessary, then, for the copies of the heavenly things to be purified with these sacrifices_, but the heavenly things themselves with better sacrifices than these. _For Christ did not enter a man-made sanctuary that was only a copy of the true one_; he

entered heaven itself, now to appear for us in God's presence. Nor did he enter heaven to offer himself again and again, the way the high priest enters the Most Holy Place every year with blood that is not his own. (NIV)

If the prime ingredient for understanding the differences between the two covenants is to locate their origins then we must acknowledge that the first was an *"....earthly copy of what was to come, "* it was never meant to be eternal (thank God!). The purpose and power of the First Covenant was for the conviction of sin by God-given *"regulation*s," It was not meant to bring a lasting atonement that would usher in the *Eternal Inheritance.* Its purpose was, and still is, to bring us, as school children, to the reality of the things that are to come, that are promised through Christ Jesus and his New (Second) Covenant.

<u>Colossians</u> <u>2:17</u> *These <u>are</u> <u>a</u> <u>shadow</u> <u>of the</u> <u>things</u> <u>that</u> <u>were</u> <u>to</u> <u>come</u>*; **the reality, however, is found in Christ. (NIV)**

<u>Hebrews</u> <u>8:5</u> **They serve at a <u>*sanctuary*</u> <u>*that*</u> <u>*is*</u> <u>*a*</u> <u>*copy*</u> <u>*and*</u> <u>*shadow*</u> <u>*of what*</u> <u>*is*</u> <u>*in*</u> <u>*heaven*</u>. This is why Moses was warned when he was about to build the tabernacle: "See to it that you <u>*make*</u> <u>*everything*</u> <u>*according*</u> <u>*to*</u> <u>*the*</u> <u>*pattern*</u> shown you on the mountain." (NIV)**

Though we have distinguished that the earthly tabernacle, and even the Law, were only copies of things to come, we must recognize that there is a relationship between the two covenants, because they are mirror images of one another. The First Covenant serves as a foundation on which the New Covenant rests, much like a house would set on its foundation. If we remove that foundation, what happens to the house? In realizing this, we know that the New Covenant is not something unattached, or alien to its predecessor, but is the fulfillment of the first. In order to understand this relationship between the two covenants, let us list out the similarities that they share:

> **1) both began with a Passover**
> **2) both require a high priest**
> **3) both require a blood sacrifice**
> **4) both have a Most Holy Place**
> **5) both have a sanctuary**
> **6) both are based on The Law**

So, if the earthly tabernacle was only a copy of the real one in heaven, then what use was it? What purpose did it serve? Paul explains it like this in Hebrews 9:9 *"....this is an illustration for the present time."* So, the purpose of the first covenant was to teach us about, and to prepare us for, the things to come (The New Order). You may ask, when will these new things come? I am not sure what all the new things are, but I do not think they will come until, as Jesus puts it, *"....until everything is accomplished."*

Again, if there seems to be these common areas in the two covenants, it is because they were meant to be mirror images of each other. It is the First Covenant that is the image in the mirror of the Second, for the Second is God eternal covenant. That is why Paul said in Hebrews 8:5 *"They serve at a <u>sanctuary that is a copy and shadow of what is in heaven</u>.."* It is here we can understand that many of the statues of the Law remain because they, too, are a reflection of the true and lasting covenant ushered in by Christ. Is there anyone who will say that the Ten Commandments are no longer valid because they are part of the Law? Or that the two greatest commandments found quoted in Matt. 26:36-40 are no longer valid because they were part of the Torah? Will the church quit asking for tithes because it is an *Old Testament* practice?

Here it would be easy to say that the Second Covenant looks like the first, so why did God bother with a New Covenant seeing that He already had described what sin is, the wages of sin, holiness etc.? There are two massive differences. The first difference is how sin is atoned for, showing that no further sacrifice would be required:

Hebrews 9:12-14 **He did not enter by means of the blood of goats and calves; *but he entered the Most Holy Place once for all by his own blood, having obtained eternal redemption*. The blood of goats and bulls and the ashes of a heifer sprinkled on those who are ceremonially unclean sanctify them so that they are outwardly clean. How much more, then, will the blood of Christ, who through the eternal Spirit offered himself unblemished to God, cleanse our consciences from acts that lead to death, so that we may serve the living God! *(NIV)***

The second difference is that the New Covenant is not only the reflection or a copy of the first (Torah) but **it** is the true and eternal covenant, thus it is the New Covenant that is the original and that has the power for eternal life. In other words, the Second (or the New) Covenant is the original and permanent Covenant; the First Covenant is/was only a (temporary) copy or shadow of the original Covenant. Thus from this we may learn that what the church has often rejected as old and outdated is really the image of the true covenant.

Now, if this seems a bit circular to you, then you are starting to understand. The two are copies of each other. Thus, the salvation of the believer is more than just *warm fuzzies*, but is a legally binding act, based on the Laws of God. If the Law is removed, then so is the legal status called redemption. The salvation of the believer is based on the Laws of Redemption as found in the Torah.

Now let us examine why the Second Covenant (the heavenly covenant) for which Christ is the mediator, is superior to the first. Even more than that, why it supersedes the First.

Hebrews 10:1 The ***Law is only a shadow of the good things that are coming*** - not the realities themselves. For this reason it can never, by the same sacrifices repeated endlessly year after year, make perfect those who draw near to worship. (NIV)

We have already come to understand that the first covenant was never meant to last, for it was always God's plan to have it *fulfill* its purpose of being a teaching *illustration of the things to come.* The first was only a *shadow* of the real one. As a *shadow*, it was powerless, with its endless sacrifices, to *"....make perfect those who draw near to worship."*

Hebrews 10:12-18 But when this priest (Jesus) had offered *for all time one sacrifice for sins, he sat down at the right hand of God.* Since that time he waits for his enemies to be made his footstool, *because by one sacrifice he has made perfect forever those who are being made holy.* The Holy Spirit also testifies to us about this. First he says: *"This is the covenant I will make with them after that time, says the Lord. I will put my Laws in their hearts, and I will write them on their minds." Then he adds "Their sins and Lawless acts I will remember no more." And where these have been forgiven, there is no longer any sacrifice for sin.* (NIV)

It is in the completion of the real (second or heavenly) covenant that we now have the *Eternal Inheritances*. This could have only come by the *fulfilling* of the *Law* and not the *abolishing* of it. Remember what Jesus said in Matthew 5:17 *"Do not think that I have come to abolish the Law or the Prophets; I have not come to abolish them but to fulfill them."* The Real has now taken the place of the Shadow, and the temporal has given way to the Eternal.

SCRIPTURE SPEAKS OF SCRIPTURE

Jesus And The Scripture

John 7:38 Whoever believes in me, as the Scripture has said, streams of living water will flow from within him. (NIV)

This is a powerful verse that is often used to tell the student of the Bible that any concept about Jesus and his teachings, or the work of the cross, must be backed up by Scripture, and with this, of course, I agree. The question is, "What Scripture is referred to here?" For the only text at the time of his statement was the Tanach (Old Testament), and yet Jesus says to believe on Him as the Scripture has said. The proof of the weakness of a Christian's Biblical education in the Scriptures can be found in his or her ability or inability to fulfill this verse. We who call ourselves believers should be able to prove the validity of Jesus as the Jewish Messiah through the Old Testament text. In fact, let me go out on a limb here and make a statement that may create some tension. It may be that our past inability to evangelize Jewish people is not based on our (Jewish) stubbornness but on the inability of Christians to prove their faith and Doctrine by the use Old Testament Scriptures. Jews are the oldest and most educated race in the world and must not be approached as if they were a Third World people. Jews make up only one half of one percent of the world's population and yet I have been told that they hold about 40 percent of all Nobel Prizes for excellence. If Jews are to be won, they must be approached from a intellectual basis that is both Jewish and Biblical. That is why Paul tells Timothy *"Do your best to present yourself to God as one approved, a workman who does not need to be ashamed and who correctly handles the word of truth."* The Old Testament is supposed to be the common ground between Jews and Christians, yet the lack of knowledge of the Old Testament by missionaries has proven to be disastrous. When the Tanach is understood, it becomes a wealth of information for the power of sharing Jesus as the Messiah. **Acts 8:35 *"Then Philip began with that very passage of Scripture and told him the good news about Jesus." (NIV)***

Preaching And Teaching

In these two verses, the Apostle Paul tells Timothy twice to continue to study the Scriptures that he grew up on, and of course the only Scriptures that were known to Timothy were those of the Tanach. Not only was he told to study, but to read the Word of God in public, and to teach and preach from it as was the custom and practice of Jewish believers for thousands of years. Paul goes on, in Second Timothy 3:16 and explains just what the purpose of the Tanach is and how to use it.

<u>1 Timothy 4:13</u> Until I come, *<u>devote yourself to the public reading of Scripture, to preaching and to teaching</u>. (NIV)*

2 Timothy **3:14** But as for you, _continue in what you have learned and have become convinced of_, because you know those from whom you learned it, (NIV)

2 Timothy **3:16** _All Scripture is God-breathed and is useful for teaching, rebuking, correcting and training in righteousness_, (NIV)

IN CONCLUSION

What is it that we have learned here? The first thing that we learned was the purpose for the Law and that purpose is to define exactly what constitutes sin. We also learned that the Law would define the conditions, basis and establish the price of redemption. Secondly, we learned that the Law has not passed away, as many have believed. In fact, for the believer, it has come to its highest apex in Christ. And in that apex, the Law has been *fulfilled*, even though not everything has been *accomplished.*

Secondly, we discovered how the Law could be *fulfilled* and yet still be in effect. If the Law has passed away, then there is no longer any definition of sin thus there is no sin. Paul said where there is no Law, there is no sin. Although we know from Scripture that Christ is the fulfillment, the Holy Spirit still has legal authority to convict the world of sin, and that conviction is through the Law. (John 16:8: *"When he comes he will convict the world of guilt in regards to sin and righteousness...."*). Because the authority to convict remains, so does the authority and power to redeem. Many Bible teachers will tell you that the Law was fulfilled on the cross, but that is only partly true. The Law is *fulfilled* one person at a time, for those who will believe and will permit Christ to be their *kinsmen-redeemer.* For them, the cross has become a fulfillment. When we stand at the Great White Throne judgment, and when all the books are open (Book of Life, Book of Remembrance, Book of the Law, etc.), our personal judgment/reward will be based on the Law (Torah). Following this time of judgment, the Law (Torah) will pass away and disappear into oblivion along with the heavens and the earth. For, like this earth, the Law is not eternal.

<u>Romans 10:4</u> *<u>Christ is the end of the Law so that there may be righteousness for everyone who believes.</u>* *(NIV)*

The third thing we have learned is that Jesus Christ is the Mediator of the New and Promised Covenant. Having brought the first to its highest apex, He alone has the right to build covenant upon covenant. The first covenant could define sin, but was powerless to make anyone righteous through its annual ritual sacrifices. But the second covenant is eternal; it brings with it the eternal offering that is once and for all. For Jesus, our high priest, has entered the Holy of Holies, and has made that eternal sacrifice, not with the blood of goats and bulls, but with His own life. This sacrifice is not only eternal, but also in the perpetual **now**, leaving no room for any other. Such a sacrifice not only atones for our sins, but also remits our sins, and cleanses our conscious from acts that lead to death. The first covenant was meant to be our Teacher and the second our Redeemer.

Our study has also revealed that as Christ has *fulfilled* the Law, there is a freedom in Christ that sets us free from the bondage of *mandatory* observance of custom and traditions of men. This freedom, however, is not freedom to follow after sin and to live in disobedience to the Word of God.

Colossians 2:16-17 *Therefore do not let anyone judge you* **by what you eat or drink, or with regard to a religious festival, a New Moon celebration or a Sabbath day. These are a shadow of the things that were to come; the reality, however, is found in Christ. (NIV)**

Let the reader understand that observing the Law for the purpose of *illustration* is Biblical, yet that observance is not to be a forced or mandatory act by which one may prove a superior state of holiness. The search for the historical Biblical Lifestyle may often take the form of practicing the Jewish Feasts and customs, for the practices and customs of the first church were Jewish. But in the zeal to recreate that historical, Biblical lifestyle, believers who choose to practice the Jewish customs and traditions must not impose them, or attempt to make them mandatory, on others.

We may not violate the very liberty that is found in the *fulfilled Law.* However, it is important that those who are Gentiles (ger-tzedeq) in Christ recognize that they are the grafted-in branches, and though they may outnumber their Messianic brothers, they are grafted to the Jewish believers and not the other way around.

As you have worked through this study, you may have found that some of your long-held opinions and beliefs have been challenged. However, we must always depend on Scripture to be the interpreter of Scripture. I have attempted to allow the Biblical Texts to answer the questions that have been raised as much as possible, and I have attempted to limit my opinion as much as possible, and not to over-interject my voice within the study. However, I shall offer up, at this time, a little of my opinion. Not on the questions raised earlier, for I believe the Scripture has answered them, but on the carelessness of some who have erroneously taught the Word of God. I do not think that I am complete or without some error, so please do more than just read this book. Test and prove the things you have learned here with your own study of God's Word.

From the time that I first became a believer, I have wanted a pure understanding of God's Word. I have wanted to be exegetical, hermetically correct. In simple language, I want to believe every line of the Scriptures, and shape my life with them. I realized early on that there is a lot of man-made teaching in the church that either refutes God's Word, or gives permission to ignore it. Such teachings have diluted the strength of the church, and have robbed it of God's presence. In many cases, the presence of the Lord has been replaced with man-made excitement. I believe that those who are called to teach the Word of God must teach the whole word, New as well as Old Testament, and that it must be taught within its cultural and historical context, not as a hodgepodge of western, post-Victorian, Gentilelized Roman paganism. To be Biblically correct is to translate the Scripture through time and culture, as well as through language.

As a result of those man-made teachings, I have noticed an almost complete disregard for the origin of the Scriptures and the context in which they were written. In my studies, I have found the Bible to be a Jewish book about a Jewish people, under Jewish Law, waiting for a Jewish Messiah. I found the loving God of Israel that opens the door to the Gentile to be grafted into *His Chosen People*, (both must have accepted Messiah). Though any believer may choose to keep the practices and feasts of the Old Testament or not, we must at the very least recognize the origin and context of our faith.

It is through Biblical Judaism that the Christians and the New Covenant Messianics have received the promise of God's grace. It is through Biblical Judaism that believers have a history and a heritage. If we deny these things, we divorce ourselves from the God of Abraham, Isaac and Jacob. And if the Church does this, into what will the Gentiles believers be grafted? For those of us who are Jews, how can we not accept the promise for which our fathers waited so long?

Finally, it is my opinion that the New Testament affirms and supports the existence, validity and relevance of the "Law" (the Torah) for the Believer of today. That means that I believe that the New Testament teaches that the law-keeping lifestyle is not only a permissible lifestyle, but a desirable lifestyle, for both Jewish and Gentile Believers as they seek to follow the Messiah. I do not believe that the New Testament **mandates** a law-keeping lifestyle, as either the means of attaining salvation, or proof of one's salvation. This issue is continuing to be hotly debated among leaders of the Messianic movement world-wide.

As with every issue related to our faith and our faith-walk, we must center our debate in the Word of God. If I have assisted the reader to dig into the New Testament portion of that Word for some answers, I have achieved my goal with this book.

GLOSSARY OF JEWISH TERMS

A-main or o-main Hebrew pronunciation of "amen"

Abba Aramaic word for father/daddy

Adonai Hebrew word for Lord

Aliyah Hebrew word for "go up." The word has several uses; to *make aliyah* means to become an Israeli citizen, also the one called to the Bima to say the blessings for the Torah reading, or to read the Torah is said to *aliyah*

Anshey Hebrew word for "people of"

Ariel Hebrew word for "Lion of God"

Ark cabinet/cupboard that holds the Torah scroll

Ark Of The Covenant a chest that was built under the direction of Moses to hold the original tablets from Mount Sinai

Aaronic Blessing Biblical blessing pronounced at the close of the Sabbath worship service, from Numbers 6:24-26

Avraham Hebrew pronunciation of the name Abraham

Bar Mitzvah / Bat Mitzvah Jewish rite of passage that declares adulthood; for young men at age thirteen, and for young girls at age twelve. Adults who convert may make Bar/Bat Mitzvah at any age

Baruch Hebrew word for "blessed"

Baruch Ha Kodesh "Blessed be the Holy One"

Baruch Haba B'Shem Adonai "Blessed is he who comes in the Name of the Lord"

Baruch HaShem Adonai "Blessed be the Name of the Lord"

Bima platform area or table designated for the reading of the Torah

Brit Hadasha Hebrew words for "New Covenant" or "New Testament"

Brit Milah/Bris Milah Jewish ritual of circumcision and naming of a new born male

Chi Hebrew word for "life," pronounced *hi*

Challah braided bread of the Sabbath; there are always two loaves symbolizing the double portion of manna which fell on the day before the Sabbath

Chumash Jewish study book of the weekly Torah portions with rabbinical commentary

Cohen/Cohenim Hebrew word meaning "priest/priests"

Cohen Gadol "High Priest"

114

Chupah/Hoopah canopy used for Jewish ceremonies that represents the tabernacle or the Word of God. A tallit is usually used as the chupah. Because of the symbolism of the tallit representing the Word of God or the Torah, activities which take place under the chupah are often referred to as occurring "under the covenant."

Day Of Atonement in Hebrew "Yom Kippur"; the 10th day after Rosh HaShanah, it is the Biblically mandated fast day commemorating the annual Day of Judgment.

Daven Yiddish for "pray"

Echad Hebrew word for "one"

El Hebrew word for "God"; one of the words used to refer to God

El-Gibbor "Mighty God"

Elohim Hebrew word referring to God, but signifying more than one, or a plurality, combined into one; a "unity"; one of ways to refer to God

El-Shaddai "All-Sufficient God"

E'man'u'el / Emmanuel "God With Us

Erev "evening"

G-d a way to refer to God with respect, based upon the Jewish tradition of not completely spelling the whole word

"God." The reason for this is to avoid taking the name of the L-rd in vain. Also, L-rd is written in the same manner

Goy/Goyim Hebrew word for "nations" or "non-Jews"

Haftorah Hebrew name for the books of the Prophets in the Bible

Haggadah the order of the Passover service; literal meaning is "the telling"

Halachah "the way to go"; post-Talmudic law; the rabbinical instruction on how to meet the requirements of the Talmud in daily living

Ha-Motzie prayer over the bread, usually the Sabbath challah

Hanukkah or Chanukah the Festival of Lights, or the Feast of Dedication; celebrating God's miracle of providing enough oil to keep the great lamp in the temple burning for eight days after the Maccabean warriors recovered Jerusalem

Ha-Shem literally "The Name"; a way of referring to God.

Ha-tikvah national anthem of Israel, literally "The Hope"

Havurah "friendship"; a get-together time of fellowship and food that follows a service

Havdalah   "separation"; the ceremony which ends the Sabbath

Kadosh   Hebrew word for "holy"

Kaddish   prayer said by the family and/or friends of one who has died

Kiddush   blessing over the wine on Sabbath and holidays

Kashrut   see Kosher

Kipa small round head covering worn by men; also called a yarmulke. It is worn to symbolize the man's awareness of and respect for God's presence and each man's responsibilities as a priest before God.

Kosher rules of religiously (i.e. Orthodox Jewish) "acceptable" food preparation, storage and eating; Biblical kosher refers to the laws of Kosher given in the Tanakh. Rabbinical kosher refers to the rules about Biblical kosher that were/are defined and expanded upon by Rabbis. Kosher is also called "Kashrut."

Ma Tovu   "how goodly"; the opening prayer of the synagogue service

Magan David   "star of David" (The literal meaning is "shield of David." Tradition says that King David used the 6-pointed star on his battle shield, so "magan David" has come to mean "star of David")

Mashiach or HaMashiach Hebrew word for "Messiah" or "the Messiah"

Matza/Matzah/Matzoh unleavened bread which is eaten during Passover and the Feast of Unleavened Bread

Menorah seven branched candlestick used in the temple; one of the primary symbols of the State of Israel. The nine-branch candlestick used for Hanukkah is sometimes referred to as a menorah also, although its proper name is the hanukkiah.

Messiah word for the Hebrew "maschiach" literally "anointed one"; translated as "Christ" in the New Testament

Messianic one who believes in a literal Messiah; generally means one who believes Yeshua (Jesus) is the Messiah.

Mezuzah a small vessel attached to the door frame of a Jewish house containing certain passages from the book of Deuteronomy. It symbolizes the blessing and presence of God in the building/room to which it is attached.

Minyan a group of 10 men over the age of thirteen who, by orthodox standards, constitute a "congregation" for purposes of some prayers/activities

Mikvah ritual cleansing or pool used for baptism

Mikamocha B'lim Adonai "Who is like you, o Lord?"

118

Mishpachah / mishpocah) "family"

Mitzvah (plural-mitzvot) commandment"; the 613 Biblical "commandments"; the "laws" of the Tanakh; can also mean any good deed

Moshe "Moses"

Nava'im "prophets"

Ner Tamid "eternal light" found over the ark/torah

Olah burnt offering; one meant to be completely consumed; dedicated to God, unrecoverable

Olam "the world", "eternity", "forever"

Oneg "pleasure" or "delight"; most often indicates a time of sharing a meal in celebration

Passover Biblical Jewish festival celebrating the Jews' release from Egyptian bondage; also called Pesach

Pentateuch the first five books of the Bible; also called the Books of Moses, or the Torah

Pesach "Passover"

Pushkah the giving- or tithe-box in a Jewish congregation

Rabbi the leader of a Jewish or Messianic congregation, similar to the pastor or minister of a Christian congregation; literally "my teacher"

Rebbe a term of endearment for one's congregational leader

Rosh HaShanah the Jewish New Year, also called the Feast of Trumpets

Ru'ach Ha Kodesh "Holy Spirit"

Sabbath/Shabbos/Shabbat the one day of the week that is to be dedicated to rest, from sundown Friday to sundown Saturday. A feast day may also be a Sabbath, even if it does not fall on a Friday or Saturday

Seder the ritual meal and story-telling of the first night of the Passover

Sefer "book"

Shach'rit the morning prayer service

Shalom "peace"; in modern usage also means "hello" and "good-bye"

Sha'lu Shalom Y'rushalay'im "Pray for the peace of Jerusalem"

Shammash "servant" or "attendant"

120

Sha'ul Apostle Paul of Tarsus

Shavu'ot spring Biblical harvest festival, celebrating the giving of the Ten Commandments to Moses

Shekinah the presence and/or the glory of God; pronounced "schkee-na"

She'ma "Hear!" Taken from Deuteronomy, this is the declaration, "Hear, O Israel, the Lord, our God, the Lord is one"; also referred to as "the watchword of Israel"

Shiv'ah literally "seven"; the time set aside for mourning the loss of a family member

Shofar ram's horn; the "trumpet" of the Bible.

Shul Yiddish term for a Jewish house of study; sometimes used to refer to a synagogue

Siddur book that contains the order of service; literally means "order"

Simcha "joy"

Sofer a scribe who is authorized to write Hebrew text

Sukkot joyous Biblical fall harvest festival, during which each family builds a small hut (Hebrew word-sukkah) attached to their house. The Bible commands that we spend a portion of each day in the sukkah to remind us of the time when the Jews lived in tents in the wilderness after leaving

Egypt. Another primary focus of the festival is God's provision for us with the harvest abundance.

Synagogue Greek word for a Jewish house of study/ prayer

Tabernacles another name for the festival of Sukkot

Tallit prayer shawl worn by Jewish men; traditionally white with blue or black threads

Talmid/Talmidim Hebrew word for "student/students" or "disciple/disciples"

Talmud the oral law; rabbinical commentary on the Tanakh

Tanach the Hebrew Bible; the Old Testament

T'ffilin the black prayer boxes attached to the worshiper's head and upper arm, used for morning and afternoon prayers; also called phylacteries

T'filla "prayer"

Teshuvah the act of repentance or "returning"; one who repents and returns to God is called "bal'shuvah" meaning "to go back"

Torah the first five books of the Bible, also called the Books of Moses; the "law"

Tzitzit the fringes of the tallit or other four-cornered garment which are meant to remind the Jew of his constant devotion to God

tzad'a'chah "charity box"

Yad the pointer used by the primary reader when reading the Torah; literally it means "hand"

Yahweh (Yhwh) the name of god, constructed from the ancient Hebrew word יהוה; the unpronounceable name of God. Religious Jews will never speak this word.

Yarmulke Yiddish word for the small round head covering worn by Jewish men, pronounced "ya-ma-ka" (the Hebrew word is "kipa")

Yeshiva a Jewish school of theology

Y'rushalay'im "Jerusalem"

Yeshua Hebrew name of our Messiah (Greek-Jesus); the word means "our salvation"

Yeshua HaMaschiah "Jesus Christ," or "Jesus the Messiah"

Yom Kippur the Day of Atonement; the last day of the "Days of Awe," which begin with Rosh HaShanah. Yom Kippur is the annual "judgment day."

QUICK REFERENCE SHEET

It is the desire of most of the traditional Christians and Messianics that I know to live as close to God's Word as possible. It has been my hope that this paper could clear up some long held myths about the Law and our Jewish roots. In order to review what we have learned, let us look at the questions that were raised and how they were answered.

Question 1) Was the Jewish Law written by men?

Answer: Exodus 31:18   When the LORD finished speaking to Moses on Mount Sinai, he gave him the two tablets of the Testimony, the tablets of stone inscribed by the finger of God.

Question 2) Did Jesus do away with the Law?

Answer: Matthew 5:17-18   "Do not think that I have come to abolish the Law or the Prophets; I have not come to abolish them but to fulfill them. I tell you the truth, until heaven and earth disappear, not the smallest letter, not the least stroke of a pen, will by any means disappear from the Law until everything is accomplished."

Question 3) What was the purpose of the Law?

Answer: Galatians 3:19   What, then, was the purpose of the Law? It was added because of transgressions until the Seed to whom the promise referred had come.

Question 4) Has God abandoned Israel and the Jews?

Answer: Romans 11:1-2   I ask then: Did God reject his people? By no means! I am an Israelite myself, a descendant of Abraham, from the tribe of Benjamin. God did not reject his people, whom he foreknew.

Question 5) Where do the Gentiles (ger-tzedeq) come in?

Answer: <u>Romans 11:17-18</u>   If some of the branches have been broken off, and you, though a wild olive shoot, have been grafted in among the others and now share in the nourishing sap from the olive root, do not boast over those branches. If you do, consider this: You do not support the root, but the root supports you.

Question 6) Must I keep the Ceremonial Law ?

Answer: <u>Colossians 2:16</u> Therefore do not let anyone judge you by what you eat or drink, or with regard to a religious festival, a New moon celebration or a Sabbath day. These are a shadow of the things that were to come; the reality, however, is found in Christ.

Question 7) Can I be saved by keeping the Law?

Answer: <u>Galatians 3:10-11</u>   All who rely on observing the Law are under a curse, for it is written:
"Cursed is everyone who does not continue to do everything written in the Book of the Law." Clearly no one is justified before God by the Law, because, "The righteous will live by faith."

Question 8) Does faith cancel out the need for the Law?

Answer: <u>Romans 3:27-31</u>   Where, then, is boasting? It is excluded. On what principle? On that of observing the Law? No, but on that of faith. For we maintain that a man is justified by faith apart from observing the Law. Is God the God of Jews only? Is he not the God of Gentiles too? Yes, of Gentiles too, since there is only one God, who will justify the circumcised by faith and the uncircumcised through that same faith. Do we, then, nullify the Law by this faith? Not at all! Rather, we uphold the Law. (NIV)